COLLECTING
ORIENTAL ANTIQUES

大清乾隆庚寅年敬造

COLLECTING
ORIENTAL ANTIQUES

Judith Moorhouse
with a chapter on ceramics by Dries Blitz

Hamlyn

Endpapers
See plate 105

Half-title page
See plate 81

Title pages
See plate 35

Opposite
1 Chinese ivory tusk carving of an immortal
or a scholar with his fan. The figure clearly
shows the original curve of the tusk. 17th
century.

Page 6
2 Porcelain vase painted in *famille rose*
enamels with floral designs on a turquoise
ground. Seal mark and period of Ch'ien-lung.

Published by
The Hamlyn Publishing Group Limited,
A division of the Octopus Publishing Group Limited,
Michelin House, 81 Fulham Road, London SW3 6RB

© Copyright The Hamlyn Publishing Group Limited 1976

Reprinted 1990

ISBN 0 600 36720 7

Phototypeset in England by
Keyspools Limited, Golborne, Lancashire

Produced by Mandarin Offset
Printed and bound in Hong Kong

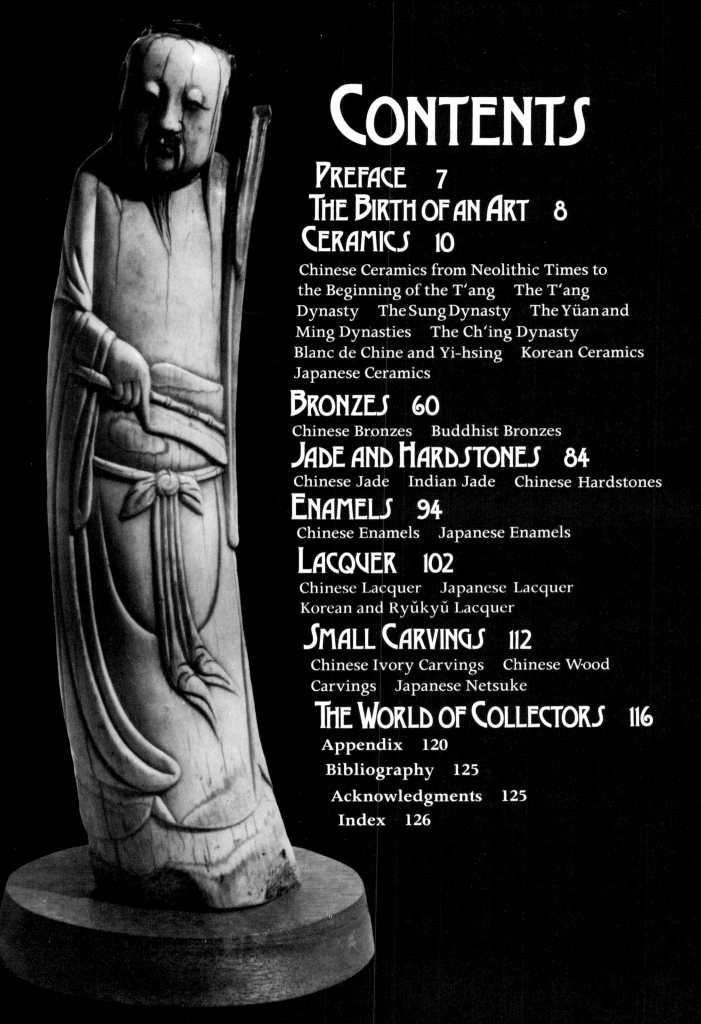

CONTENTS

PREFACE

The wealth of antique objects of art stemming from the Oriental cultures accommodates easily a wide range of tastes which are not necessarily just those for 'the mystical Orient', 'chinoiserie', Samurai swords or the like. Western concepts of art and good taste can as easily be brought to bear in the appraisal of blue and white porcelain as of Wedgwood china or Myers silver.

However, unlike much artistic achievement in the West, Oriental art can pose problems for the collector. On the one hand, the anonymity of some craftsmen presents a void rather than a frame of reference; and on the other, the wealth of imitations of earlier styles together with misleading date marks or copies of signatures may provide so much conflicting evidence of date or period that the collector finds himself completely perplexed.

Thus it is only to be expected that a guide to the collecting of Oriental antiques must discuss stylistic and technological developments against a background of the societies which engendered them. The reader will pinpoint the areas which conform most closely to his personal taste, or inspire him to interest in an artefact or form of decoration previously outside his experience.

At the same time he will develop an objective appraisal of the artistic merits of each class of objects. His reading will acquaint him with the development of the ceramic arts—the characteristic wares of each historical period, their techniques of construction and their decoration; the working of bronze in all its forms, and its peculiarities of shape and design; the qualities of jade and hardstone; the intricacy and labour of lacquer and enamel, and the wealth of small carvings for which the East is renowned.

The objects discussed are but a selection of the enormous range of artefacts extant and represented in major collections, museums and dealers' showrooms throughout the world. In this small volume many have had to be omitted, but it is hoped that the reader's encounter with those discussed will impel him along the path trodden by so many other Westerners to the world Oriental antiques.

Incidentally, it is interesting to note that the majority of the pieces illustrated have been on sale in the art market during the last ten years.

Judith Moorhouse

THE BIRTH OF AN ART

Art and technology have been intimately associated since primitive man's first successes in toolmaking. Indeed, the word 'technology' comes from a Greek stem meaning 'art', that is, human skill as opposed to nature. Early man had a need for elementary tools and vessels, and the progression from the use of flints and bones to metal-tipped tools and projectiles, and from horns, shells and gourds to primitive pottery, was an obvious one, given the wit to take advantage of natural materials such as clay, copper and tin. During this period of development, spanning some thousands of years, the main requirements for domestic objects were established, and have remained essentially the same ever since. Implements for hunting, cultivation and defence complemented man's entire needs.

Once the range of required objects had been established, the slow process of improving the methods by which they were made commenced. The dramatic shift from hand fashioning to the potter's wheel and from crude casting of arrowheads to the casting of whole vessels came about. At this stage the regional migration of knowledge and techniques began to play a critical part, enabling the pace of development to sharpen. Nevertheless this did not prevent the retention, often for centuries, of a particular advanced technique solely within a relatively enclosed ethnic area, the production of porecelain in China being an example. The more complex the technique, the more the operation of the craft would become the prerogative and only occupation of a group trained solely for it. The cultivators and the hunters would continue their specialised activities but the cadre of craftsmen would standardise the application of proved techniques and continue the search for new ones. Moreover, the production of objects in general domestic use would begin to require quicker, simpler and less costly methods.

But what of art in all this? To pose such a question is to suggest that the basic human need for respect and reward for creativity, or the personal need to explore the realm of inventiveness, are not natural instincts at all. It was inevitable that once the frontiers of utility had been crossed all future developments would be an amalgam of function, technique and decoration, the purposes for which the object was made deciding the relative importance of these components. Some vessels would be respected for their beauty rather than their use, indeed

might never be used as vessels at all. Their decoration and their craftsmanship would begin to exist for their own sakes.

Man's advance in the organisation of his society and the employment of natural materials, animals and elementary tools brought in its wake the need for further technological development. The harnessing of a chariot team with leather thongs necessitated metal rings or clasps to protect the parts subject to most wear, and the wood chariots required metal protection at key points such as the axle caps. Inasmuch as pride or competition would be a powerful factor influencing the craftsman, the creation of a new object of utility would be followed immediately by its embellishment. Thus the owners of chariots would command respect not only for the power of their teams, not only for the construction of their chariot and the metal with which it was reinforced, but above all for the decoration of its bronze fittings. It can be seen that the chariot owner was as much dependent on the artistry of the craftsman as the craftsman was on the patronage of the owner.

'Patronage' is inevitably a loose term. For the sake of discussion perhaps it may be classified as 'minor' patronage and 'major' patronage. Minor patronage in the sense of the rich man's requirements of his local potter or metalworker, or the demands of minor chiefs or potentates for functional or decorative objects to be met at the level of technology, materials and craftsmanship locally available. The craftsman, in turn, would endeavour to stimulate the demand for his wares by improving on existing types, or promoting orders by gifts of his work.

'Major' patronage has probably been the impetus for the colossal dimension of Chinese art and craftsmanship. It could only occur in circumstances of a strong central authority, perhaps exercising control over the type of objects produced, the motifs, decorations and colours, and even the way in which craftsmen were trained. Entitlement to this absolute power was apparently justified by the volume of work commissioned, work that gave employment to a vast staff of craftsmen in workshops or factories. The factories may have been established by the authority itself, as were the imperial kilns during the Ming dynasty. Moreover, central authority and patronage of this kind was a magnet attracting the best artists, not only from provinces under the authority's control but also from beyond its frontiers. A further advantage to the craftsmen under imperial protection and support would be that rare materials, such as cobalt blue or cinnabar colourings, would be exacted as tribute from distant states, or could be purchased with the wealth of the patron.

The relationship between patron and craftsman was thus defined as of mutual advantage and was not to change significantly thereafter. The range of objects required, in terms of their utility, was virtually complete, new requirements being limited to objects for decorative rather than practical use. Eventually it becomes impossible to improve the balance and effectiveness of a sword blade, but scope remains for its handle and scabbard to be embellished, such decoration providing the criterion by which one sword is judged superior to another.

The relative merit of an object changes from its being esteemed for its effectiveness of function to its being admired for its style or wealth of decoration, the transformation being complete when its utilitarian function is abandoned and it assumes a purely decorative or ceremonial one. A stylisation and de-utilisation with very early roots is the regeneration of forms and decorations of vessels and icons for religious practices, such as archaistic bronzes and Buddhist figures. But the dominating example of stylisation and decoration for the sake of art is without question the science of ceramics in China. Moreover, the respect for traditional art forms and the pursuit of art for its own sake led to interest in collecting, and, in turn, to the production in China of illustrated albums of craftsmanship of a former period, as early as the 10th century AD.

The circle of reinforcement in which better materials led to better craftsmanship, better craftsmanship sought patronage, patronage attracted rare materials, rare materials encouraged superior decoration, superior decoration engendered decrease of function, and decrease of function enabled yet further craftsmanship for art's sake, could only be broken, contained as it was within one culture, by external influences. These were dramatically provided by Europe's expansion to the East. Europe's enormous demand for the production of export wares, often to a lower quality, was responsible for the manufacture of articles with Western designs. For better or for worse, this gave the craftsman an opportunity to participate in a large external market and to loosen the bonds of patronage.

See plate 20

CERAMICS

Chinese Ceramics from Neolithic Times to the Beginning of the T'ang

The history of Oriental ceramics begins in China, at least as long ago as the 5th millennium BC. Here, in the basin of the Yellow River in what is now Honan province, were made the first known Chinese pottery objects of artistic interest.

There are two main styles in the pre-dynastic period. The products of the Yang Shao culture are the earlier and have a robust and often 'primitive' appeal. The pieces are generally made of reddish clay which was fashioned by hand in strips—so-called coils—and sometimes finished on a slow-turning potter's wheel. Early examples have simple forms with painted or impressed designs using red or black pigments and often representing animals or fish; occasionally human faces are shown. The decoration is extremely stylised and to the modern observer is sometimes reminiscent of Picasso paintings.

To the west of Honan, in Kansu province, we find a later development of this culture with pottery shapes that are more sophisticated. Vessels with a decoration of scrolling geometric designs are typical of this group. The pieces are often surprisingly light in weight and the majority of them have been found in graves, buried with the dead. It is therefore likely that many of the designs on them have a symbolic meaning which cannot now be understood.

The Yang Shao culture was replaced by the Lung Shan culture. In the past there has been much speculation among archaeologists as to the historical sequence of these two cultures, but it has now been established from excavations that the Lung Shan culture falls between Yang Shao and the first historical period in Chinese history, the Shang dynasty. Like the Yang Shao people, the Lung Shan were farmers and fishermen, but they had an important technological advantage in the fast-turning potter's wheel. Their pots, which are often black or dark brown with a burnished surface, may have quite thin walls. The shapes too differ from the previous culture's, displaying an advanced potting technique.

Of course, pottery was also made in other parts of China, but the two types described here are the most distinctive. In south-eastern China, for example, a somewhat cruder grey pottery was made.

During the Shang dynasty (1600–1027 BC) ceramics never rivalled the magnificent bronzes of the period, though ceramic designs owed much to them. The influence of the preceding Neolithic tradition also continued to be strong, with the use of impressed designs, often of a 'basket-work' pattern made by pressing a piece of woven material into the still-wet clay before firing. There were, however, important technological innovations. For the first time, a pure white firing clay—kaolin—was used; and so was a high-fired glaze, perhaps of felspathic type. The latter required a kiln temperature of about 1200°C. before it would fuse, resulting in a ware with a hard smooth body—stoneware.

The Shang tradition persisted in the Chou period (1027–475 BC) and indeed it is sometimes difficult to distinguish between the products of the two dynasties. Glazed pieces are rare, and it would seem that the art of making high-fired glazes was temporarily lost. By the 8th century BC a type of glazed ware had appeared in Anhui province, but it was inferior in quality. It was only just before the Han period that lead glazes on earthenware bodies came into use, heralding a long lead glaze tradition, culminating in the splendid and colourful wares of the T'ang dynasty.

It is appropriate here to define the three main body materials:

Earthenware is usually red to grey in colour and fired up to a temperature of about 600–1000°C. The clay may be refined, but it is not mixed with other materials and is porous. It may be covered with a lead glaze to render it

3 Earthenware urn with scroll design in black pigment. A funerary vessel dating from the Yang Shao culture, from Kansu province. Neolithic period, late 3rd millennium BC. Gemeentemuseum, The Hague.

Ceramic centres of the Far East

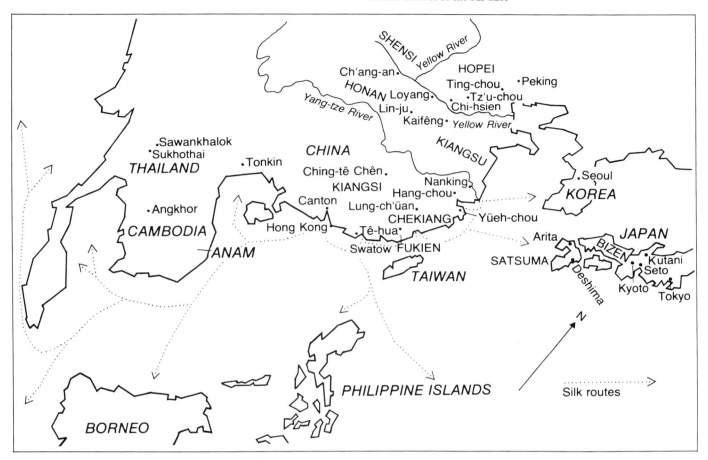

impermeable. Lead glaze contains sand or quartz (silica) and uses lead-oxide as a flux; it is fired at the relatively low earthenware temperatures and therefore cannot be used on stoneware or porcelain unless they have first been fired up to their proper temperatures.

Stoneware is much harder than pottery and usually grey in colour; it is non-porous and not translucent; and it is fired at temperatures ranging from 1100 to 1300° C. The body is made up of clay and China stone or 'petuntse'. It may be covered with a felspathic type of glaze that can withstand high kiln temperatures.

Porcelain is hard, white in colour with a fine-grained texture, non-porous and translucent; it is fired from 1150 to 1350° C. and usually covered with a felspathic type of glaze. The body is also mixed in that the main ingredients are China stone (petuntse) and China clay (kaolin). As glaze and body share certain ingredients (petuntse), they fuse together superbly well. Flaking, as found on pottery, is totally absent. The Chinese do not make a distinction between stoneware and porcelain, whereas in the West body colour and translucency are used as criteria to distinguish between the two.

It is fortunate that so much pottery has survived from the Han period (206 BC–AD 220). As well as being artistically valuable, it provides us with a fascinating insight into daily life in Han times. Many of the pieces were excavated from tombs, and the range of objects found is astonishing, from bowls and vases and utilitarian wares of all sorts to animal figures, soldiers, servants and even architectural models of farms, watch-towers and granaries. The tradition of *ming-ch'i*–burial of objects with the dead–began in the Han dynasty as a replacement of the earlier custom of human sacrifice, and the tombs have yielded not only pottery effigies and utilitarian products, but also wood, silver, jade and bronze pieces. Food and drink were also provided for the dead person. Since the nobility was declining in influence under the Han, richly furnished tombs were no longer almost exclusively aristocratic, but might belong to high ranking civil servants or army commanders. After all, the founder of the Han dynasty was a commoner, and the old ideals of the Chou aristocracy had lost much of their meaning under a dynasty whose emperor–the Son of Heaven–was but an ordinary man.

Although unglazed pottery pieces were made in quantity, it is clear from the tomb finds alone that the use

11

4 Earthenware model of a horse with detachable head. For these pieces the legs were made of wood and fitted into slots on the underside of the body. Unglazed with traces of pigmentation. Han or Six Dynasties, 2nd to 4th centuries AD.

5 Earthenware *hu*, covered with a green lead glaze. An imitation of a contemporary bronze example. The shoulder has hunting scenes in relief. *T'ao-t'ieh* masks are also often found on this type. Han dynasty. Victoria and Albert Museum, London.

of a lead glaze was now widespread. Pale amber and green lead glazes are commonly found; the vessels are often based on contemporary or archaic bronzes, and it is thought that the green glaze was intended to imitate the patination on bronzes. The modelling of the figures and animals is less stylised than in previous periods; the Han potter strove for greater realism, with results that are sometimes quite lifelike. Often a sense of humour can be detected in the rendering of animal or human form.

5   The green-glazed vessel shown here is a direct copy of the bronze *hu*, with rings moulded on the body instead of hanging loose from the animal mask; the shoulder has a moulded frieze of animals. On such lead glazed pieces the glaze has often decomposed so that it is covered with a silvery surface not unlike the iridescence on Roman glass.

Of far greater significance for the development of ceramics is a class of ware that began to be made around the 4th or 3rd century BC in Northern Chekiang province

6   on China's east coast. This was Yüeh ware, named after the principality near the Yang-tze river mouth, and made at the Chiu-yen and, later, at the Shang-lin hu kilns. It has a grey body and is covered with a greyish green or olive green glaze of felspathic type. It is often undecorated, although moulded or incised ornament of flowers or birds does occur. It was made until the beginning of the Sung dynasty and is often called the forerunner of the Chekiang celadons which were made in Sung times at Lung-ch'üan and other kilns. It was regarded very highly by scholars and connoisseurs in China, especially during the T'ang dynasty, and reached its peak about the 10th

century. Yüeh ware was the first of the long line of celadon wares made in both northern and southern China. The term celadon is applied to a broad group of wares in which a greyish stoneware body is covered with a greyish green to olive green glaze that may or may not be transparent.

The Six Dynasties (AD 221–589) saw the spread of Buddhism, which had come from India at a time when the old values of the Han were being challenged. China was in continual trouble with nomad tribes invading the country, and the most successful of them founded the Northern Wei dynasty (386–555). The iconography of Buddhism, with its many deities, gradually began to appear in Chinese art, at first mainly in stone sculpture.

6 Stoneware jar covered with an olive coloured celadon glaze. The rim has iron brown spots. The base is concave and shows traces of kiln supports. Yüeh ware. Six Dynasties.

7 Earthenware stallion with rider, unglazed, with traces of pigmentation. The rider is of non-Chinese origin, probably from western Asia. Northern Wei period.

Sculpture had never been really widely practised in China before, but it became more popular now, and this was naturally reflected in pottery figures. The horse shown here is a big stallion, representing the kind of beast that originated in western Asia and had been sought after in China since Han times. The Chinese succeeded in breeding fine horses, and this animal has impressively noble features. Its rider is probably of western Asian origin. The grey earthenware is covered with a powdery slip to which unfired pigments were added, usually to indicate harness trappings, facial features and other details. As these colours were not fired in a kiln they have largely disappeared, usually leaving only a few traces.

During the Six Dynasties, lead glazed pottery, so popular during the Han dynasty, did not re-emerge until

8 Two earthenware musicians. Usually a group of musicians would be made from the same mould with the different instruments added separately. Traces of polychrome pigmentation. T'ang dynasty.

8 Two earthenware musicians. Usually a group of musicians would be made from the same mould with the different instruments added separately. Traces of polychrome pigmentation. T'ang dynasty.

the 6th century, a fact so far unexplained. China was re-united under the short-lived Sui dynasty (581–618), in which there was an increased use of *ming-ch'i* and an almost colourless lead glaze made its appearance. The modelling of burial figures became even more naturalistic and is often close in style and conception to that of T'ang products.

The T'ang Dynasty

The period that followed the Sui dynasty is often regarded as the most splendid and opulent in Chinese history. Under the T'ang dynasty (618–906) China was ably governed from a central capital, Ch'ang-an, which was one of the most cosmopolitan cities in the entire world. The famous 'silk route' to western Asia and the Middle East, pioneered in Han times and afterwards neglected due to wars, was re-opened by powerful Chinese armies. Foreign traders were welcomed in China, and many of the ideas and objects they brought were copied and adapted. And as China now embraced such a large area (including Tibet and Korea) the capital was thronged with foreigners, including entertainers summoned to amuse the emperor and his court.

The T'ang potter had now achieved such control over firing and glazing techniques that the burial wares at times rival the objects fashioned from jade, silk and precious metals. (These, however, give an indication of the sheer opulence of T'ang life that the pottery cannot.) However, T'ang domestic life was the most common subject, vividly depicted in pottery often decorated with brightly coloured glazes. The flowering of T'ang polychromy was in the first half of the 8th century, and there are many fine examples in museums throughout the Western world. It must be noted however that virtually all figures were made in moulds in multiple sections, though they were sometimes individually finished. Large numbers may therefore be found with identical features, and charming though most of the figurines, animals and other representatives of daily life may be, they may justifiably be regarded as mass-produced. The glazes are of great interest. They were often intended to copy woven materials, and in many cases the glaze falls short of the base of a vessel or figure. This is quite deliberate and may represent the folds or edges of cloth, the splashed colours on the 'material' being in imitation of coloured designs. It has in fact been suggested that the batik method of dyeing cloth—with

16

resistant wax or grease preventing the dye from taking in selected areas–may also have been used on T'ang polychrome pottery.

A rich family in mourning showed off its wealth by putting expensive burial objects in the tomb of the deceased, a practice that became so extravagant that the court issued decrees regulating both the size and the number of pieces allowed according to rank. Many of the larger pieces such as vases are monumental in appearance. They are constructed from many separate pieces, luted together, and embellished with applied, incised or stamped ornament. Some shapes and decorative elements show western Asian influences, Sassanian or Greek, brought along the trade routes. Laden camels with camel drivers were favourite subjects for the T'ang potter, and of course many examples of the famous T'ang horses were made.

These pieces were made in large numbers and they have also been unearthed in quantity from tombs. Apart from grave robbers, the Chinese respected their ancestors too much to seek out the tombs and empty them of their treasures. Only in the early years of this century, when Western engineers laid railroads across the country, were numerous tombs discovered. Many pieces found in them are still obtainable by collectors. Of course prices have risen sharply in the past decade but the output was so prodigious that a relatively wide choice is still available. However the collector has to be careful–especially with unglazed ware–since modern fakes are quite common, and some of them are very good imitations indeed. The glazed wares pose less of a problem because the genuine glaze tends to have a crackle with a very fine mesh which has developed over the centuries and is very hard to imitate. (This is not to say, of course, that genuine pieces with wide crackled glaze do not exist.)

The long history of porcelain began about this time. Europeans struggled to discover the formula for porcelain until the 18th century, but the Chinese made it during the T'ang dynasty and possibly even earlier. Perhaps the earliest porcelain is *hsing-yao*, a ware described in early Chinese texts; but the kiln sites, thought to be in Hopei, have not so far been located. The typical bowls and ewers often have rolled rims and a flat base, the bowls usually with a recessed circle in the centre. Sometimes the almost colourless glaze was applied over a white slip. (A slip is a coating of liquid clay that is used either for decoration or to cover up roughness or unsuitable body colour, caused by mineral impurities.) Sherds of this ware have been found at Samara, the old capital of the Islamic empire, which was abandoned in 883. Some authorities argue that the birth of porcelain did not take place in northern but in southern China, and perhaps as early as the 6th century.

Obviously the discovery was of enormous importance to ceramic history. In fact, *hsing-yao* may be called the prototype of the later *ting-yao*, one of the celebrated white porcelains of the Sung period.

The Sung Dynasty

The fall of the T'ang was followed by the period of the Five Dynasties in which the country was divided between rival warlords. In the meantime China had been forced to give up her possessions beyond the old borders and the trade routes to western Asia had been cut off. The reunited China of the Sung dynasty (960–1279) was smaller and less secure than T'ang China.

The first Sung capital, Kaifêng, was perilously near the Liao kingdom (907–1125), which had sprung up on China's north-eastern border; in fact the Chinese had to pay the Liao rulers large sums to keep them at bay. This situation lasted for many years, during which the Liao kingdom came increasingly under the cultural influence of China. Then the Liao rulers were overthrown by the Chin, a vassal state which ruled the former Liao empire between 1115 and 1234. When the Sung emperor tried to take advantage of this development, the attempt

10 Earthenware flask, shaped in imitation of a leather example, covered with a pale green lead glaze. Liao dynasty.

failed disastrously; his armies were defeated, Kaifêng was taken in 1126 and the emperor, with a large part of his court, was deported to the north. Thus ended the Northern Sung dynasty (960–1127). In the south, however, a son of the former emperor was proclaimed emperor and, after years of fighting, a pact with the Chin was signed. Hang-chou became the capital of the Southern Sung dynasty. The end came when the Mongols arrived from Central Asia and, having defeated the Chin, overthrew the Southern Sung in 1279, founding the Yüan dynasty.

While under the T'ang China had been outward-looking, dynamic and in search of expansion, people in Sung times had a more inward-looking and contemplative attitude towards life, often harking back to the achievements of their ancestors. This was reflected in some of the applied arts, although perhaps less in ceramics than in jade and bronze. Whereas T'ang ceramics impress with their sometimes massive and elaborately constructed forms and highly coloured glazes, at times bordering on vulgarity, the Sung potter achieved an all-pervading subtlety in his means of expression. He sought to represent nature and her harmonies, and the majority of his forms were based on flowers, especially the lotus. In decorating surfaces he exercised great restraint; colours of glazes are generally muted and usually of monochrome type; carved, combed, incised and moulded designs were generally executed in low relief. The main wares of the Sung dynasty will be discussed in two parts: those of the north and those of southern China.

Northern wares

Ting ware. Perhaps developed from *hsing-yao*, this is a 29 porcelain with a finely grained body, displaying an orange glow when held against the light. The glaze, applied direct to the body, is ivory in tone and runs in drops ('tearmarks') away from the rim, which is usually unglazed because the pieces were fired upside down, perhaps to prevent them from warping. The base is glazed, as is the foot rim, although exceptions occur. Plain types are attractive and available to collectors, but the ware is more famous for its pieces with incised, moulded or carved decoration, usually consisting of flowers or birds and animals. The rims of bowls and dishes are usually copper-bound. Red, black and purple varieties are extremely rare. *Pai-ting* (white Ting) is the finest in quality, *t'u-ting* (earthy Ting) being an inferior, coarser type.

Northern celadon. A stoneware with a greyish body, 11 covered with a transparent olive coloured glaze. Similar decorative techniques and motifs to those on Ting

wares were used although the style is often bolder and more energetic. The glaze has many bubbles and, where exposed, the fired body exhibits a deep brown colour. The ware was made over a large area of northern China, Yao-chou and Lin-ju Hsien being the best-known kiln centres. As with Ting ware, the plain types are more common and collectable.

28 *Chün ware*. This stoneware is covered with an opalescent, lavender coloured glaze varying in tone. Where exposed, the body is a deep brown colour. The range of shapes is smaller than that of most Sung wares, and pieces are usually small. The thick glaze forms the only decoration in the earlier pieces, but the later ones sometimes bear relief designs. On later types there may be suffused purple streaks in the glaze. The ware was made well into the Ming dynasty, to which a group of bulb bowls, with numbers (1–10) incised in the base according to size, perhaps belongs. Made in Chün-chou district in Honan, as well as at many other kilns, Chün ware was

12 Stoneware jar with deep brown to black glaze on which is painted abstract floral decoration in a lighter tone of brown. Northern brown ware (Honan type) of the Sung dynasty.

copied in the 18th century, especially in Kuangtung (Canton) and Yi-hsing near modern Shanghai. A green glazed variety, green Chün, also exists.

12 *Northern brown wares.* These are also called 'Honan' type wares. Black and brown glazed stonewares were produced at a large number of kilns in northern China. Some of these kilns are known to have produced Tz'ŭ-chou wares as well (see below). The stoneware body is coarse grained and buff in colour, covered with a thick brilliant deep brown or nearly black glaze on which designs may be painted, usually of an almost abstract floral type, in a lighter tone of brown. Pear-shaped bottles and bold massive jars with narrow short necks and wide shoulders are well known forms. A copy of the Chien ware teabowls was also made. Bowls and bottles with 'oil spots' (small purplish or silvery spots) are a much sought-after type, but are rarely genuine.

3,14 *Tz'ŭ-chou type.* A stoneware with a coarse grey body on which a range of decorative glazing techniques was used. Pieces are often large, with bold decoration and forms. There are four basic glazing methods:
(a) The body is covered with a white slip to render it suitable for painting. A design, usually floral, is painted on in brown or black and covered with a thin transparent glaze.
(b) A design is cut through the white slip so that the darker body stands out against the white overall slip, under a colourless glaze (sgraffito technique).
(c) A design is cut through a dark glaze before firing and so stands out in buff against the dark overall glaze.
(d) Designs are painted on a colourless glaze in green enamel and iron red. This may be the earliest use of overglaze enamel painting.
Sometimes a turquoise or green glaze is substituted for a colourless glaze as in technique (a). The painted designs are more reminiscent of 'folk art' than anything else in Chinese ceramics. The type was made in the Tz'ŭ-chou district in Hopei province but also in many kilns in other parts of China. The ware is still being made today.

Southern wares
Chekiang celadons. This is the stoneware most readily associated with the term 'celadon'. The products of the
15 Lung-ch'üan kilns and other kilns such as Ch'u-chou were exported throughout South-East Asia, and also reached the Middle East. The body is pale grey in tone and covered with a thick opaque glaze that may vary in colour from deep olive to greyish blue. Where exposed, the body turns a deep brownish red colour in the kiln. As the glaze is opaque the decoration is simply carved or applied, lacking the strength of detail of the Northern celadons with their transparent glazes. Slip decoration

14 Pillow with slightly curved top with lotus carved under the bright green lead glaze. Tz'ŭ-chou type of the Sung dynasty.

also occurs towards the end of the Sung period and later. The tripod censers, lotus bowls (with rows of petals, carved or moulded in relief on the outside) and dishes at best have several layers of glaze giving a beautiful depth to the colour. The bluish variety is much sought-after, especially in Japan, and is sometimes called 'Kinuta'— which is inconvenient as 'kinuta' is the Japanese term for a mallet-shaped vase with two handles which was a popular celadon shape. The centre of small dishes may have a decoration of two fish in relief swimming in opposite directions. These are sometimes called 'bridal dishes', twin fish signifying marital bliss. Celadons were made throughout the Ming dynasty and the heavy dishes with moulded and carved floral designs found much favour with Indian and Middle Eastern courts on account of the belief that they would change colour or crack if poisoned food was placed in them. A type called Li-shui was derived from Yüeh ware and, having a transparent glaze with carved designs, may be sometimes confused with Northern celadon. Lung-ch'üan types have been and are imitated (in Japan), but the imitations are usually made of white porcelain rather than grey stoneware.

Chien ware and Chi-an ware. Chien ware is a stoneware with a coarse dark brown or black body covered with a thick, lustrous glaze of varying brown tone suffused with bluish black streaks. On the tea bowls—conical bowls with unglazed rims—the glaze collects in pools in the centre and, on the outside, stops short of the foot in thick drops. These bowls were very popular in Japan from the 13th century onwards, becoming known as 'temmoku' bowls. This name is also given to the Northern Brown ware teabowls and to Chi-an teabowls. Chien ware was made in Fukien province.

Chi-an or Kian ware is best-known for variants of Chien ware teabowls, but the body is buff and (unlike Chien wares) the glazes may have figurative designs. Sometimes an actual leaf was used in the making of the floral designs. Tortoiseshell was imitated by superimposing a lighter coloured glaze upon a deep brown glaze. Kian ware was made in Kiangsi province, whence its name. White wares reminiscent of Ting ware were also produced there.

33 *Ch'ing-pai type.* This was made over a wide area of China and is a white porcelain. The name refers to the colour of the glaze and not to any particular kiln; it means 'bluish white'. Wares of this type are also known as *ying-ching* ('shadowy blue') and were exported all over South-East Asia. They were made in enormous quantities and are still quite common. There is a large range of shapes and the pale blue to white glaze often covers carved, incised or moulded decoration, usually of floral subjects. The later types are sometimes fired on the rim of the mouth like Ting ware. The pieces are generally thinly potted, and flower-shaped bowls often have nicks on the rim to indicate lobes or petals. Although some pieces with a white glaze may resemble Ting ware they never have its creamy texture or its teardrops. *Ch'ing-pai* wares were probably made well into the Ming period. One centre of production was Ching-tê Chên, the later ceramic 'capital' of China.

Ju ware and Kuan ware. These wares really fall outside the scope of a book for collectors, since they are among the rarest of Chinese ceramics. Very few pieces of the beautiful Ju ware are known to be in private collections, so it can only be seen in museums. It was an imperial ware of the Northern Sung dynasty, made in Honan only between 1107 and 1127. The first date is found on a test ring in the P. David Foundation in London; the second is that of the fall of the Northern Sung dynasty. The body is greyish and is covered with a blue-grey crackled glaze. It was usually fired on 'spurs' (kiln supports) which leave marks on the base.

Kuan ware was an imperial ware of the Southern Sung dynasty. Its body is dark brown and covered with a very thick glaze that is crackled and varies in colour from grey to pale blue. It was made near Hang-chou, the capital, and was extensively copied, especially during the later reigns of the 18th century. The forms of both Ju and Kuan wares are based mainly on those of bronzes.

Ceramic wares of interest were made in the Liao kingdom itself. The Liao potters carried on the T'ang lead glaze tradition but employed shapes that were
10 inspired by their own nomadic metal and leather vessels. The flasks with wide bellies and wedge-shaped necks or mouths covered with brightly coloured glazes—mainly green, yellow and brown—are typical examples of the Liao style. The glaze colours tend to be lighter in tone than those of the T'ang, and the body material generally has a pinker tinge. White porcelains have been found in the Liao region, but as yet little is known about their production. It must be remembered though that the kilns at Ting-chou were not far away from the borders of the kingdom, so not everything found there is necessarily the work of Liao potters.

16 Stoneware tea bowl covered with a thick brown glaze with blackish streaks that stop short of the foot. Chien ware of the Sung dynasty.

17 Stoneware jardinière on tripod feet and covered with a glassy celadon glaze. The ornament consists of the 'Eight Trigrams'. From Chekiang province, early Ming dynasty.

18 Porcelain stem cup painted in underglaze cobalt blue with dragons, the interior with dragon decoration in low relief. Yüan dynasty, first half of the 14th century.

The Yüan and Ming Dynasties

During the Yüan period (1280–1368), China was ruled by the Mongols, who started up a flourishing foreign trade again. Most of the kilns that had been active during the Sung dynasty continued production although in certain wares a coarseness in quality became apparent. Far more important was the development, if not the introduction, of porcelain painted with underglaze cobalt blue pigment–the famous 'blue and white'. This involved painting on the designs when the piece was dry; afterwards it was covered with a colourless glaze and the whole process was finished off in a single firing. The technique was not invented in China; during the 9th century potters in Mesopotamia used cobalt oxide to decorate their wares, though it was applied on a white tin glaze, and during the 13th century potters in Kashan in Persia used cobalt blue decoration actually painted under the glaze. The blue glazes found in T'ang ceramics apparently played no role in the development of Chinese blue and white. Oddly enough, although cobalt ore was imported from Persia, there are few designs in Chinese blue and white which can be related to Persian examples.

Although some authorities believe that the introduction of underglaze blue painting in China took place under the Sung dynasty, the more widely accepted view is that it did not occur until the late 13th century. The classic period for blue and white was the early Ming and especially the early 15th century. It was not until this period that the Chinese began using native cobalt ore. The porcelain first used for painting in underglaze blue was of a type similar to the Shu-fu ware of the Yüan dynasty, the first official ware (that is, ordered for the court) which was made in Ching-tê Chên, a town in Kiangsi province that was to develop into a ceramic metropolis. This ware was often decorated with raised designs in slip under the glaze, sometimes incorporating the two characters 'shu' and 'fu' ('central palace'), which is how it got its name. It was probably developed from ch'ing-p'ai ware, and these two porcelains formed the bases for the earliest blue and white.

Painting on porcelain in underglaze copper-red was also developed, but because of technical difficulties a large number of pieces 'misfired' and the desired pinkish colour was not achieved. The usual reason for failure was an unstable reducing atmosphere in the kiln. Iron oxide was also experimented with although not much is known about wares so decorated. Most pieces were small and painted with simple floral designs; many of them have been found in the Philippines and Indonesia. Jarlets with similar decoration in underglaze blue and

red as well as designs in iron brownish red shows that the Chinese potter was experimenting, but so far no pieces have been found in circumstances indicating a Sung date of manufacture. In the early period the range of shapes and decorative motifs gradually widened, although their development was hampered by a tendency to regard them as vulgar – understandably in the case of a court sensibility formed by acquaintance with the subtle Sung monochromes.

Two pieces are crucial for the dating of early blue and white, since both bear dates corresponding to AD 1351. They are two tall vases with elephant-head handles in the Percival David Foundation in London. The acceptance of this date provided a key to the study of early blue and white, showing what an impressive development it had undergone in such a comparatively short period. The style of drawing is sure, bold and imaginative. Typical features are the spiky leaves, dragons with small heads, and the bold style of wave and border patterns. The deep blue often has blackish spots where the pigment was too liberally applied, causing it to sink into the glaze (the 'heaped and piled' effect) and to burn black in the firing. Colour is generally not a good criterion for dating as it is always liable to vary considerably. Large vessels and plates were now being made, and they all display a comparable energy in their decoration. In some cases,

exact contemporary copies of blue and white pieces exist in copper red; however, the technical difficulties mentioned above caused copper-red ware to disappear from the scene from the late 14th to the 17th centuries.

To many collectors the apex of ceramic art is reached in the first half of the 15th century. Blue and white has come of age; the young, energetic and bold style has matured into one of balance and symmetry which has not lost too much of its former vigour. The decoration is now arranged to fit the shapes better, and certain decorative elements are more stylised. The large dishes with flat unglazed base are typical of the period. The painted leaves are more rounded, and the whole decoration is kept under supreme control. There is a good range of forms, and the superb glazes have a characteristic surface that has been likened to orange peel and may be slightly bluish in tone.

It is not until the time of the Hsüan-tê emperor, the fifth ruler of the Ming dynasty, that reign marks are found on porcelain. Some pieces exist with the reign mark of the emperor Yung-lo (1403–24), but although many pieces are attributed to his reign, the marked pieces are not accepted as 15th century. A typical Yung-lo type is a conical bowl which may be incised under the glaze or may have underglaze blue decoration. Floral designs are now supplemented by landscapes often showing sages or officials with mountainous scenery and trees forming the background. The 'landscapes' in the earlier (14th-century) pieces often consisted of scattered flowers or shrubs surrounding the central figures.

The names of Chinese emperors were not their own but were chosen upon ascending the throne.[1] The reign mark is usually written in two vertical groups of three characters reading downwards and from right to left, the third and fourth characters being the title of the reign. Comparatively speaking, many pieces that were undoubtedly made in the 15th century have survived bearing the Hsüan-tê reign mark. Sir Harry Garner, a world authority on Chinese art, feels that only a small proportion of Hsüan-tê marked wares were actually made in this short period (1426–35), the rest belonging to the period between 1436 and the beginning of the Ch'êng-hua reign (1465). Other authorities believe that all the 15th-century Hsüan-tê marked pieces belong to the reign; they attribute the unmarked pieces in similar style to the Yung-lo reign, whereas Sir Harry Garner assigns a large number of these to the Hsüan-tê reign.

In 1465, the Ch'êng-hua emperor ascended the throne

[1] These names are in fact descriptive reign titles rather than proper names. Until the Ming dynasty such titles were chosen for certain years within an emperor's reign, but thereafter one reign title only was adopted for the duration of a reign.

of the 'Middle Kingdom' after years of great political unrest. The porcelains made during his reign show marked differences from those of the earlier 15th century. Very large pieces which were previously common were now less often made, and the style of potting and decoration is more delicate and elegant. The imperial wares became ultra-refined with delicate potting and superbly smooth glazes that tend to have a slightly yellowish hue—although this is virtually imperceptible when viewing a piece by itself—in contrast to the bluish cast in the glazes found on the more robust earlier pieces. The 'heaped and piled' effect is hardly ever seen and the underglaze blue colour is silvery in tone and delicately shaded.

The artist's choice of decorative media was widened by the introduction of a new technique, called in Chinese tou-ts'ai ('clashing colours'). In this the important areas of the design are painted in pale underglaze blue outline, and enamel paints in subdued colours are used to complete the design. The enamels have to be fixed in a second firing. Among the best known examples of this style are the delightful 'chicken cups' showing a hen and chicks in a garden.

There are many other decorative motifs at this period, from the flower scrolls and fruits on the famous 'palace bowls' (bowls about 6 in. in diameter with continuous bands of flowers or fruit in underglaze blue) to landscape designs with children at play and also Buddhist and Taoist motifs. In the design and the quality of the porcelain, they rank among the best wares that China has ever produced. The 'orange peel' effect has largely given way to a silky smooth texture, making handling a piece a delight. The marked pieces of this period usually have the mark written rather carelessly and in a watery tone of blue.

The Ch'êng-hua reign probably also saw the introduction of the celebrated 'Imperial Yellow' which was to become the imperial tableware. The yellow may vary from a very pale tone—as often found in the Hung-chih period (1488–1505)—to a brownish hue in the reigns of the later Ming period. It is not simply a yellow glaze but a yellow enamel superimposed on an already fired piece with a transparent glaze. The result is a very pure yellow, unaffected by impurities in the body underneath, but because the temperature of the second firing is rather low the glaze may easily be scratched and rubbed—which often happened. The base is always white, in other words only covered with a transparent glaze. The range of shapes is limited, consisting mainly of bowls and dishes of varying though standardised sizes. The tradition of using yellow monochromes for the court persisted until the end of the Ch'ing dynasty, though in the 18th century the technique of two glazes was replaced by one using only a single yellow glaze.

In ceramics the change from the Ch'êng-hua to the succeeding Hung-chih period is gradual and often imperceptible. Among the finest wares of this period are the dishes painted in underglaze blue with a floral spray and a yellow background filled in and fixed by a second firing. Also generally assigned to the Hung-chih reign is the 'windswept' group—somewhat coarse vases and sturdy wine jars, decorated in underglaze blue and showing figures in a garden with robes flowing as if blown by the wind. These pieces have unglazed bases

with shallow rounded footrims, and the body contains many iron impurities. Yet another type of ware has a design of dragons reserved in biscuit—that is, not covered by the transparent glaze—and this is covered with a bright green enamel which is fixed in a subsequent firing. The type continued to be produced during the rest of the Ming period. At times, pieces occur with designs left in the biscuit stage, which means that for some reason the green enamel was never applied. Pieces with underglaze blue decoration bearing the Hung-chih

20

20 Porcelain saucer dish with five-clawed dragons enamelled in green on the biscuit. Mark and period of Hung-chih. Victoria and Albert Museum, London.

mark are extremely rare while the other types are usually marked.

The following emperor, Chêng-tê, was rumoured to have become a Moslem, and indeed there are a number of pieces, decorated in underglaze blue, which bear his reign mark and have either Persian or Arabic inscriptions. There is no proof that Chêng-tê ever did become a Moslem, but we do know that Moslem eunuchs at his court had considerable power. It has been suggested that the pieces with Near Eastern inscriptions may have been made for these eunuchs, who would have been conversant with Arabic for religious purposes. These 'Mohammedan' wares have reign marks consisting of six Chinese characters, while other blue and white wares are notable for having four-character reign marks. The glaze often has a greenish tinge, and by 15th-century standards the designs are crowded. In many cases, however, the quality of the drawing is excellent. A form of decoration popular during the early 16th century was painting with polychrome enamels alone, usually red, yellow-green, aubergine and turquoise. The mark may then occur in iron red.

An entirely separate group of wares is the *fa-hua* type, where the potter tried to imitate cloisonne enamel. The 'cloisons' are formed by shallow ridges of clay which separate the medium-fired enamel colours, forming a design. The pieces may be either stoneware or porcelain, and are sometimes massive in size; they often have floral designs or landscapes with figures as their decoration. The usual colours are dark blue, turquoise, aubergine, green and yellow. Sometimes the design is cut out of the walls of a vessel in openwork.

The Chia-ching emperor who succeeded Chêng-tê tried to stamp out corruption amongst the court eunuchs,

21 Porcelain jar painted in underglaze blue with the 'Three Friends' signifying the three great religions of China as well as the virtues gentlemen should have. Mark and period of Wan-li.

22 *Fa-hua* bowl with lotus flowers outlined with raised fillets of clay, covered with aubergine, yellow and blue glazes. Early 16th century.

who had become very powerful. Being fanatically devoted to Taoism, he decreed that Buddhist images and emblems were no longer to be used; that is why Taoist iconography and imagery occur so frequently on Chia-ching porcelain. The blue and white wares of this period are renowned for the violet-purplish intensity of the blue although not all pieces display this characteristic. Drawing, potting and glazes are still excellent on the best pieces, but the majority, though attractive, display a measure of carelessness in execution and finish. The bases of bowls and dishes are often concave, in contrast to earlier pieces which usually have convex bases. Apart from the ubiquitous dragon and floral decoration, the Eight Taoist Immortals often occur; so do the 'Three Friends' (bamboo, prunus and pine issuing from rocks), although this particular design was popular throughout Chinese history. 'Shou' characters (long life) are shown in the form of peach trees (themselves emblems of longevity) with their trunks contorted to form the actual character. The Taoist God, Shou Lao (also known as Lao Tz'u), is often shown, flying on his crane or accompanied by a deer holding a piece of fungus in its mouth.

In the 16th century the Chinese potter had an astonishing range of decorative techniques at his command, and demand for his products was tremendous. In the year 1544 over 100,000 pieces of porcelain were ordered for the court alone, and the number of non-imperial pieces would most certainly have been far greater. The reign of Chia-ching saw the start on a large scale of the direct export of wares, in the first instance to the Portuguese via the port of Macao near Hong Kong. A number of pieces bear Portuguese coats of arms although these have merely been added to purely Chinese designs, a fact that suggests they were only adapted in a superficial way for the export market.

The short reign of the Lung-ch'ing emperor produced porcelains that but for the reign mark would be virtually indistinguishable from the preceding or succeeding reigns.

A typical product of the Wan-li reign is *wu-ts'ai* ware so called because the term *wu-ts'ai* means 'five colours' Here the range of enamel colours is wider than on *tou-ts'ai* wares, and the design tends to be outlined in either black or red rather than underglaze blue. However, the underglaze blue still forms part of the decoration. Although many pieces lack the technical excellence of earlier wares they possess an enchanting and at times breathtakingly 'wild' and baroque vitality.

The export trade continued to boom. The Portuguese now had to face strong competition from the Dutch; and vast quantities of porcelains, possessing great charm, found their way to Europe in Portuguese 'carracks' and their Dutch counterparts. This type of ware, called 'Kraak' porcelain, is well potted and painted in a

23 Porcelain dish with underglaze blue decoration. This export type, the so-called 'Kraak' porcelain, was western Europe's first direct import from China. Late 16th or early 17th century.

silvery tone of underglaze blue, usually with rustic animal scenes surrounded by shaped panels with flowers or fruits. Deer, birds on rocks, water plants and insects, all sketchily but charmingly rendered, are standard decoration. Dishes and bowls with fluted rims were common and can often be seen in 17th-century Dutch still-life paintings. The dishes have a coarse finish, with sand adhering to footrim and base. Radial lines on the base – 'chatter marks' – often show that the potter was careless when cutting the footrim of the piece.

They are perhaps indicative of the speed with which these porcelains were turned out.

In Fukien another ware was made, also for the export market. Swatow wares – named after the main port from which they were shipped – show similarities in design to the porcelains made at Ching-tê Chên, but they have more deficiencies in finish and virtually all pieces have sand adhering to the base and footrim. Apart from examples in underglaze blue, designs were made in white slip on a pale blue, celadon or chocolate brown ground;

enamelled types are also common. Most of the designs changed little.

Monochromes were fairly rare in the 16th century, but combinations of glazes occur more often. Yellow designs on a green ground, and gilded decoration added to red, purple or blue glazes, are found especially during the Chia-ching and Wan-li reigns; the latter are known as 'Kinrande' wares. Porcelains of the reign of T'ien-ch'i, although often technically rather poor, were exported to Japan in particular, where the small saucers—round, fan-shaped or square—could be used for the tea-ceremony. The decoration, either floral or with charming scenes of birds or animals, is like that of Wan-li export pieces in its sketchiness.

The Ch'ing Dynasty

The Manchus—a Tartar race from Manchuria—exploited the internal unrest in China to invade the country and set up their own dynasty, the Ch'ing (1644–1912). Once again China was torn by war, with the Manchus taking over from the north and vigorous Ming resistance in the south which it took many years of fighting to suppress. The ceramic factories of Ching-tê Chên suffered heavily from these upheavals. Although the Manchu rulers actively supported the arts, their military preoccupations prevented them from supporting the manufacture of imperial porcelain until 1682, when a new commissioner of the imperial factories arrived from Peking.

However, production had not ceased in the meantime. Between the end of the T'ien-ch'i period and 1682 the factories, temporarily released from imperial influence, made porcelains with an unmistakeably new character
24 and flavour. These 'Transitional' wares—produced during the period of transition between Ming and Ch'ing dynasties—show great individuality in conception and decoration. Forms are usually elegant, and the porcelain itself is very refined and covered with one of the most superlative glazes to be found anywhere in Chinese ceramic history. The pieces were painted in underglaze blue of violet tone. They usually have scenes taken from ancient stories—often well-painted landscapes with horsemen—while borders are always of a floral nature. The earlier pieces have stylised tulips as border designs; the tulip was immensely popular in Europe, and especially in Holland where, during the years of the 'tulip craze' in the 1630s, fortunes were paid for tulip bulbs. The smooth glazes of Transitional wares are of a slightly greenish hue, while the body itself is pure and white and heavily potted, although never clumsy in shape. One salient feature of the decoration is the representation of grass by V-shaped brushstrokes; another is the 'clouds' used to separate scenes on the same lateral band.

During the same period *wu-ts'ai* decorated pieces were also often made, a very popular form being large baluster-shaped jars with massive covers. A curious 'outsider' is a ware with a deep blue monochrome glaze, usually covering a design of dragons chasing pearls among clouds. These are heavily potted bowls with flared sides and brown rims, and all have the base covered with a dark brown slip. The dragons are often scraggy looking beasts, reminiscent of those found on Wan-li pieces.

During the reign of the K'ang-hsi emperor, we see the emergence of a new porcelain, superbly refined and distinctly different from the Transitional wares. In these carefully potted and finished objects there is nothing to remind us of the perfunctory finish of late Ming wares.

They were the products of a new and well-organised division of labour applied to porcelain production. Père d'Entrecolles, a Jesuit priest who lived in Ching-tê Chên in the early 18th century, sent letters to Europe with fascinating descriptions of the production process. Not only was the material itself worked on by several individuals at different stages – often even the decoration was executed by more than one artist.

In view of the many individuals involved, the harmony of the end-products is surprising. The many shapes are masculine; the curves and angles are generous but never sloppy or weak, and pieces always rest on a firm, well-potted base. The bases of nearly all K'ang-hsi porcelains have 'pin-pricks' – tiny, unevenly spread holes in the glaze. A large amount of blue and white was made,

painted in a strong hue applied in overlapping washes. The style is more elegant in conception than before, although some pieces are lacking in individuality; but generally speaking form and decoration are finely balanced. K'ang-hsi marked pieces are rare, and usually Ch'êng-hua, Hsüan-tê or Chia-ch'ing reign marks are to be found.

,43   The main enamelling style employed on porcelain during the K'ang-hsi period is called *famille verte* ('green family') because of the extensive use of green enamel. The enamels are those found in the *wu-ts'ai* of the Ming period, but a greater clarity of tone is achieved and the red is rather thinner.

During this reign a new enamel colour was introduced. This was a fine translucent blue, initially used in com-

bination with underglaze blue, which it later replaced altogether on enamelled porcelain. Technically it was a difficult colour to produce satisfactorily and on many fine *famille verte* pieces the blue is disappointing. A typical feature is the 'halo' of dulled glaze surrounding the blue.

Enamels were also applied direct on to the fired 36 porcelain (biscuit); the chief colours used were green, purple, aubergine and yellow, with designs drawn in black. Monochromes of this type were also popular. The enamelled and blue and white pieces are decorated with extremely varied subject matter, from the purely floral to extensive landscapes with or without fishermen, boating scenes, mythological beasts, and historical court scenes derived from prints. Borders are usually panelled

26 *left* Shallow earthenware dish supported on loop-shaped tripod feet. The central medallion was stamped into the clay and then glazed. The design is influenced by Sassanian metalwork. *right* Amber glazed earthenware jar. Both T'ang dynasty.

27 *left* Earthenware horse covered with a pale straw-coloured glaze. A typical feature of this group is the outstretched stiff front legs. Sometimes pigments were added to the glaze. Sui dynasty. *right* Earthenware horse covered with a dark brown glaze with parts glazed yellow. The saddle is unglazed. T'ang dynasty.

28 *left* Shallow stoneware dish with upturned rim covered with an opalescent pale blue glaze. Sung dynasty. *centre* Pear-shaped stoneware bottle with pale-blue glaze and purplish splashes. Yüan or early Ming dynasty. *right* Small stoneware offering dish with thickened rim, covered with an opalescent pale blue glaze. Sung dynasty. All three pieces are Chün ware.

29 Shallow porcelain dish with moulded design of a dragon surrounded by flowers and foliage. Ting ware of the Sung dynasty.

30 Roof tile ornament: a rider on horseback standing on a curved base and covered with polychrome glazes. Probably 17th century. Chinese domestic architecture favours buildings of low, often single-storey, height. Thus the embellishment of the roof with brightly glazed figures was, and still is, very popular.

31 Two porcelain bowls with everted rims, painted in underglaze blue with court scenes. The bowl on the right has an interior border of swastikas, a Buddhist symbol. Both K'ang-hsi period.

32 *left* Porcelain bottle with ogee-shaped landscape panels in underglaze blue reserved on an underglaze 'powder blue' ground. *right* Small porcelain mug with underglaze blue decoration of 'long Elizas'. Both K'ang-hsi period.

33 Porcelain bowl with finely carved lotus flowers and covered with a pale blue glaze. *Ch'ing-pai* ware of the Sung dynasty.

left Stem cup with design in *tou-ts'ai* enamels. *right* 'Chicken cup' also with *tou-ts'ai* decoration. Both of the Ch'êng-hua period. *top* 'Chicken cup' with similar decoration but of the K'ang-hsi period. Percival David Foundation, London University.

35 *left to right* A *famille verte* porcelain basin with ladies in a garden. A salt, a direct copy of a European example. A deep cup. A plate with birdcage hanging from the branch of a tree; the flat everted rim was a concession to European forms of tableware and was for condiments. K'ang-hsi period.

—the panels are often ogee-shaped—and floral grounds were popular. A large quantity of fine quality wares was made for export and it is sometimes not easy to tell these from wares made for the home market. In general the 'Chinese taste' wares are more sparsely decorated and have no borders. The conventional imperial designs dating from the Ming dynasty were still made, and the court continued to favour the designs that featured the dragon and the phoenix. Among the great triumphs of the reign were monochromes which reached an unsur-

passed level of technical excellence and inventive artistry.

Sang de boeuf, or ox-blood, is the famous red glaze — derived from copper—which on the best examples resembles the colour of crushed strawberries. In later pieces suffused streaks of blue or purple occur (*flambé*). The K'ang-hsi version of this ware, which already existed in early Ming times, is usually called Lang-yao after a certain Lang, whose identity has never been established but who was thought to have been respon-

63

sible for the production of this ware. The colour is usually pale near the lip, and the base may be either white, crackled or of a celadon colour. The glaze is usually thick, and there are variations in tone on a single piece.

Celadons, often with carved decoration in low relief, were also made – at Ching-tê Chên – and have a porcelain body (unlike the stoneware Ming celadons, made at Ch'u-chou in Chekiang province). These celadons, and also turquoise, yellow and aubergine glazed porcelains, were very popular, finding their way into French castles and homes sometimes 'enhanced' by French ormolu fittings. There is a profusion of shapes, and, as in Ming times, figures were popular, especially those of the biscuit group of wares. A very rare colour is the *clair de lune*, which is the most delicate shade of lavender blue. Later in the reign the superbly refined 'peachbloom' glazes appeared. These were reserved for use on eight objects, all small and all intended for the scholar's table. The waterpots of beehive form are the best known, with three delicately incised medallions showing archaistic

37 Porcelain dish with 'Imperial Yellow' glaze. Mark and period of Hung-chih. Private collection, London.

38 Large porcelain fish bowl decorated in *wu-ts'ai* style with mandarin ducks swimming in a lotus pond. Wan-li period. Victoria and Albert Museum, London.

39 Porcelain saucer dish with landscape design in polychrome enamels. Early 16th century.

dragon motifs, all under the pinkish-red glaze, with darker and lighter spots and occasional flecks of green. The slender amphora-shaped vases are among the most refined of monochromes.

A variant of the *famille verte* group is decorated with *famille verte* enamels but on a ground of yellow (*famille jaune*), green or black (*famille noire*). There has been much speculation about the authenticity of the large vases and jars with black grounds, which appealed to American collectors early in this century and are well represented in American galleries. Another innovation was a very shiny black glaze called 'mirror black', often enhanced by mythical beasts in gilt. A delightful green monochrome is called 'apple green', which consists of a green enamel applied over a crackled glaze, thus producing a 'soft' appearance. *Famille verte* enamels can also be found in panels surrounded by a 'powder blue' ground, a variant of underglaze blue blown on to the paste through a bamboo tube with a piece of gauze at the end.

The early 18th century saw the introduction of a new enamel, the *famille rose* (pink). Its name comes from the pink enamel which is the dominant colour and which is derived from gold. From about 1720 this was to be the most important of the enamelled palettes, though *famille verte* continued to be made, at times in combination with *famille rose*. *Famille rose* colours stand out more above the glaze than *famille verte* colours and unlike them are distinctly opaque. They were also more easy to handle and therefore facilitated the development of a new painting style in which the execution tended to be more meticulous. There is a group of bowls, with *famille rose*

decoration on different coloured grounds, that bears the K'ang-hsi mark and in all probability belongs to the period. The rose is far from perfect and is obviously only in its early stages of development. This enamel colour is non-Chinese in origin, having been introduced from Europe by a Jesuit priest.

Several of the glazes described here were invented by Ts'ang Ying-hsüan, director of the imperial factories in Ching-tê Chên, or have at least been attributed to him. It was he who in 1683 supervised the rebuilding of the imperial factories after their destruction during the commotions of the early Ch'ing period. He and his successors, Nien Hsi-yao (1726–36) and T'ang ying (1736–53), were largely responsible for the running of imperial factories, which in turn heavily influenced the multitude of private kilns in and around Ching-tê Chên.

Nien Hsi-yao was director during the reign of the Yung-chêng emperor (1723–35), and while he was in office porcelain became more and more refined. It became fashionable to make copies of the classic wares of the Sung dynasty, such as Kuan and Ju ware. 15th-century blue and white was also extensively copied but the painting is too deliberate and the porcelain too white to deceive. The 'robin's egg' glaze (bluish green glaze with flecks) was also introduced at this time.

But above all the period is famous for *famille rose* wares, from which all traces of technical immaturity had now disappeared. The artists exercised superb control over the enamels, and the 'rose' can be seen in a marvellous variety of shades, from very pale pink to a fine vibrant ruby red. Drawing is excellent and on the best pieces is rendered with a delicate touch that is most apparent on pieces made for the home market, with their sparse decoration set against a white ground. The export pieces tend to be overcrowded; the best example of this is perhaps a group of plates with seven heavily ornamented borders and a ruby-coloured back. A certain amount of Ching-tê Chên porcelain was sent by boat to other places, such as Canton or Peking, to be decorated. Ladies with children, and peony and peacock designs, are among such decorations and are often seen in Western collections.

The most famous of the three directors at Ching-tê Chên was T'ang ying, who took over from his predecessor in 1736. He had a thorough knowledge of the craft of porcelain-making; in fact he had been Nien's assistant, and it has been said that some inventions made in Nien's time were the work of T'ang. He was a prolific writer too, producing several books about the manufacture of porcelain.

It is hard to describe the best wares produced at this time. The enamelled pieces express more of the individuality of the artist/studio-potter, and some porcelains are so thin as to be described in the West as 'egg-shell'. One

of the innovations of the Ch'ien-lung reign is the 'tea dust' glaze—a double glaze in which the green enamel is blown through gauze on to a yellow ground, giving a pale, soft, mottled greenish brown effect.

One of the most remarkable achievements of Chinese potters was their ability to imitate other materials, such as bronze, gold, silver, jade, lacquer, bamboo and wood. Foreign styles and objects were also extensively copied. Japanese Imari ware, Italian albarellos (drug jars) and Italian glass were among the types successfully copied.

What was in fact happening was that artistic inspiration was giving way to an obsession with technique—a tendency that eventually led to artistic decline. Designs became monotonous and at times even vulgar. The potter tried to show off too many of his technical skills on a single piece, overcrowding it, or producing an effect of over-exuberance and garishness—in short, bad taste. Even rose enamel lost its delicate appearance and became muddy and heavy.

Monochromes were still made in quantity, and a feature

42 Porcelain model of the deity Chên Wu seated on a throne with an acolyte on either side and tortoise with snake at his feet. Turquoise and blue glazes with the faces left in unglazed biscuit. 16th century.

43 Porcelain dish painted in *famille verte* enamels with pheasants, rocks and flowers. K'ang-hsi period.

44 Porcelain figure of the goddess Kuan-yin, on a rockwork throne.
Blanc de Chine, from Tê-hua in Fukien province. K'ang-hsi period.

often encountered is a fine crazing (crackling) of the glaze, often only visible under magnification. It had now become common practice to mark porcelain with an archaic seal script, and the six-character mark was no longer used very often. Blue and white wares became less popular, and those still made were often copies of 15th-century types. Complete services were made for export, sometimes with European coats of arms (*chine de commande*), and the shapes were—naturally—Western.

A European influence appears in a porcelain perfected under T'ang's supervision. *Ku-yüeh Hsüan* ('ancient moon terrace') is a very finely enamelled type of porcelain made for the palace; the European influence appears in the handling of perspective and light and shadow. Most pieces were marked with seal marks in blue enamel and are small in size. The technique originally came from glass enamelling but the name is also applied to porcelain.

The long and internally peaceful reign of the Ch'ien-lung emperor favoured the arts; but in the first year of his reign, Ch'ien-lung's son, Chia-ch'ing, was faced with a revolt. Lacking his father's wisdom and intelligence, he was unable to cope effectively, and the Ch'ing dynasty began to decline as revolts and external pressures multiplied. Over the years that followed, porcelains became more and more debased, though fine pieces were still occasionally made; an attractive group is that of 'graviata bowls' which bear circular panels with landscapes or floral designs on a coloured ground that is finely incised with floral scrolls. But often potters chose unhappy combinations of colours, while the colours themselves became harsher in tone. The quality of the actual porcelain also deteriorated, and after the reign of the Tao-kuang emperor a majority of the wares were of a poor standard. However, it is worth repeating that there are exceptions and that some 19th-century wares are certainly well worth collecting.

Blanc de Chine and Yi-hsing

The porcelains discussed in the last two chapters— imperial and non-imperial—came from Ching-tê Chên in Kiangsi province. There are also two provincial kilns that should be mentioned: one producing *Blanc de Chine* at Tê-hua in Fukien province, and the other, a Kiangsu kiln, producing *Yi-hsing* brown stoneware.

The earliest *Blanc de Chine*—white porcelain with a clear glaze—probably dates from the 16th century. The range of forms is quite large, but the best-known pieces are figures of deities, officials and merchants. The ware itself is outstanding because of its superb body material, a fine clay which is very translucent and smooth to the touch. The glaze fits the body very tightly, and the body and glaze form a union unrivalled anywhere else. The colour varies from bluish white to a warm ivory tone with a pinkish tinge.

The great plasticity and strength of the Tê-hua clay enabled the modeller to use it in unusual ways. Extremely sharp edges and fine details could be obtained, allowing the artist great freedom; and the tightness of

49

46 Stoneware teapot. *Yi-hsing* ware from Kiangsu province. 18th century. Victoria and Albert Museum, London.

the glaze meant that the details did not become blurred. A great variety of figures was produced, notably Buddhist, Taoist and other religious deities. The most famous of all is undoubtedly Kuan-yin, the goddess of mercy, who may be seen in a variety of poses and was a popular subject throughout the history of *Blanc de Chine*. There were also Kuan ti, the god of war and literature, Lohans and many others. Unidentified officials are also common, their austere expressions and clothing lending them a not at all unpleasant aloofness. In the early figures, heavy potting and fire cracks are usually present. Dating *Blanc de Chine* is difficult; styles persisted over many years, and colour of glaze is no guide at all. Potting and artistic excellence are generally the most important considerations in dating.

There is also a good range of bowls, plates, cups and vases in *Blanc de Chine*. In these the body and glaze are the same as those of the figures, and for both groups moulds have been used in the manufacturing process. Perhaps the best-known of the utilitarian wares, for example, are cups made in imitation of rhinoceros horn,

which have been moulded and afterwards embellished with separately moulded relief decoration – usually prunus, peach and deer, dragon, tiger or stork. When these pieces are viewed against the light, one sees a glow that may vary from pinkish cream, through white, to a greenish colour. Another group consists of pieces made after European examples. Most Western collections and museums contain examples of teapots, wine cups – sometimes double-walled, with an openwork outer wall – and also mugs, jugs, vases and beakers, often with the applied and separately moulded decoration.

Yi-hsing ware was and still is made in Kiangsu province near Shanghai. The material is a brownish-red unglazed stoneware that sometimes has a burnished appearance. The ware itself often bears small marks in the form of seals. It is believed that the kilns started in the 16th century, and *Yi-hsing* is well known in the West, where modern teapots in the ware are admired for the excellent tea that can be made in them. To most of us, teapots, in a variety of forms, are what *Yi-hsing* is all about. Yet there are other wares such as delightful imitations of fruits

50

47 Korean stoneware *mei-p'ing*, incised with lotus flowers under a crackled greyish-green celadon glaze. 12th or 13th century, Koryō dynasty. Korean ceramics sometimes show strong Chinese influences, but in boldness of shape and execution of decoration they are typically Korean.

48 *left to right* From Korea, small brushwasher, pear-shaped vase, and shallow oil jar. All three pieces show a decoration of inlaid flowers in white and black slip under the celadon glaze. This is a decorative technique not found in China. 12th or 13th century, Koryō dynasty.

and bamboo, and there is also a glazed variety of *Yi-hsing* made in imitation of *Chün-yao*. The teapots are difficult to date for the same reason as *Blanc de Chine*: forms and decorative styles persisted over long periods of time. Engraved or applied low relief decoration (usually floral) is common, and the variety of subject 30,49 matter is not great.

Korean ceramics

Although Korea was under the political and cultural 47 influence of China for much of her history, her ceramic art nevertheless displays an independent character. Dating from the Silla period (57BC–AD 936) a well-known type is a grey, usually unglazed stoneware with firm, sometimes angular shapes and incised, stamped or carved ornament. Natural (wood-ash) glazes are occasionally found on these pieces. Justly famous are the delightful celadon wares of the succeeding Koryō period (936–1392) with their handsome forms and decoration carved under the glaze, painted in iron brown under the glaze or inlaid with 48 black and white or coloured slips. The latter is a decorative technique which is peculiar to Korea from

which later on the wares with brushed slip decoration were developed. The celadon glazes vary in colour from the common greyish blue to a brighter 'kingfisher' blue. A refined and rare white porcelain was also produced. The Yi period (1392–1910) saw a decline in technical standards, but the designs found on the iron brown, copper red and underglaze blue decorated wares can have a tremendous impact due to the vigour and freshness of their brushwork. The accurate dating of many Yi ceramics is still a problem. The rustic qualities of the Yi wares greatly influenced Japanese potters, and Korean Yi shapes and decorative elements can be found in Japanese wares made for the home market, for instance those produced for the tea ceremony.

Japanese ceramics

It is always difficult to discuss the ceramic art of Japan without inviting comparisons with China; and indeed in some periods the Japanese potter owed a great deal to his Chinese counterpart. But there are too many examples of Japanese originality to justify the notion that their art is simply one of imitation.

49 Three pieces of Thai stoneware: a globular jar, covered with a crackled celadon glaze; a deep dish with incised ornament and celadon glaze; and a box and cover with brown glazed ornament on a buff ground. Sawankhalok ware. 14th or 15th century. Although many Thai ceramics must appear crude in comparison to their Chinese counterparts, they have a certain earthy vitality and are now gaining in popularity.

In prehistoric Japan—about which we know very little—a type of pottery was made that is known as Jomon ware. Strong forms were achieved by pounding coils—strips of clay—into shape, and impressed rope patterns were a frequent mode of decoration.

The use of the potter's wheel is evident in the later Yayoi pottery, which is roughly contemporary with the Chinese Han period. The shapes of this ware are generally smoother and more sophisticated, and engraved patterns occur. This type underwent further development from about AD 300 to AD 600, the 'Tomb Mound' period (so called from the custom of marking tombs by building large artificial mounds of earth over them). The Haniwa figures are the most striking products of the period, with impressive sculptural qualities; the lower part always consists of a hollow tube—to be placed in the mound of earth—while the top half represents a human or animal figure with features roughly cut out in a very modern-looking style.

From the 8th century the Japanese court at Nara maintained friendly relations with T'ang China, and many Chinese artefacts were imported and copied. Another import was Buddhism, which now became the main religious force in Japan. The Japanese have always been renowned for the way in which they preserve their treasures, and in the Shōsōin storehouse at Nara there are a number of pieces—ceramic and otherwise—that demonstrate the strength of Chinese influence on Japanese artists of this period.

By the early 10th century, intercourse with China had been interrupted. For several hundred years Japanese potters were left to develop their own styles, although later on potters at the Seto and other kilns started making imitations of various Sung wares, notably the Lung-ch'üan celadons and also brown-glazed wares.

The famous tea ceremony gave rise to a great deal of ceramic production in Japan. The Japanese got their taste for tea from China, and the brown glazed bowls of Fukien province (Chien ware) were especially admired and copied. The ceremony itself originated with the Zen Buddhist sect who regarded its ritual as a useful aid to the process of meditation; but later on it became a cult in its own right. Originally very much an upper class observance, the tea ceremony eventually became popular with the middle classes, greatly stimulating the demand for objects associated with the ritual. Not only tea bowls

50 Earthenware 'Haniwa' figure of a seated woman with details carved in the clay. 4th–6th century. National Museum, Tokyo.

51 Porcelain bottle with underglaze blue decoration. Arita ware. 17th or 18th century.

52 Porcelain figure of a lady, her robes painted with Kakiemon enamels. Arita ware. Second half of the 17th century.

53 Porcelain vase painted with flowers in Kakiemon enamels. Arita ware. Late 17th century. British Museum, London.

but also incense burners and containers, flower holders, water containers and tea jars were needed. Potters at kilns such as Seto and Bizen settled down to meet the demand, making pieces which, whether glazed or unglazed, almost always reflect the Japanese taste for a 'rustic' look in pottery. The most celebrated of all these objects were the Raku wares—low-fired bowls of a deceptively simple appearance (it should always be remembered that this rustic simplicity of form and glaze was the premeditated achievement of a skilful potter). These pieces were usually covered with lead glazes, yellowish or brown or black in colour.

The southern island of Kyūshū played an important role in Japanese ceramics. Here a settlement of Korean potters made pieces reminiscent of the wares made in Korea from the 14th century onwards. This type, called Karatsu ware, has simple floral designs painted in iron brown under the grey glaze.

In the 17th century porcelain began to be made on Kyūshū. The town of Arita became a centre of production, for the kaolin needed to manufacture true porcelain was found near there. The first Japanese porcelains exhibit a strong Korean influence, with simple designs of birds and plants sketchily drawn in underglaze blue. The shapes are pleasing, but the quality of the porcelain is rather poor by comparison with contemporary Chinese wares. This group of wares is not often seen in the West as collectors have tended to concentrate on later 17th-

54 Two porcelain jars and covers from a garniture set, painted in underglaze blue enriched with bright enamels. Imari type, Arita ware. Late 17th century.

51 century products of Arita.

Because of shortages of supply in China, Dutch traders sought an alternative source of ceramics in Japan. In 1641 they were allowed to establish a trade mission on the tiny island of Deshima, just outside the port of Nagasaki. Chinese export wares were now copied at Arita kilns, and soon pieces clearly intended only for export were produced, with shapes that were entirely European. The underglaze blue decoration, however, is a rather curious adaptation of late Ming and Transitional originals. The blue tends to be inkish in tone, although a strong violet tone also occurs. The glaze usually has a texture resembling orange peel.

About this time (the second half of the 17th century) a new style of enamel painting was introduced – according to tradition by the Kakiemon family, after whom it is named. In Kakiemon ware we see a form of decoration 53 that is Japanese in origin, in its typical form with a superbly controlled use of space, sparse decoration and designs that are asymmetrical without being unbalanced. The main subjects for decoration were flowers and animals; song birds on branches and fire birds were particularly popular. The enamels are turquoise, blue, green, yellow and iron red. The porcelain itself is very refined and white. Much admired in Europe, this ware was extensively copied by factories both on the Continent and in England.

It would be difficult to find a greater contrast to

57

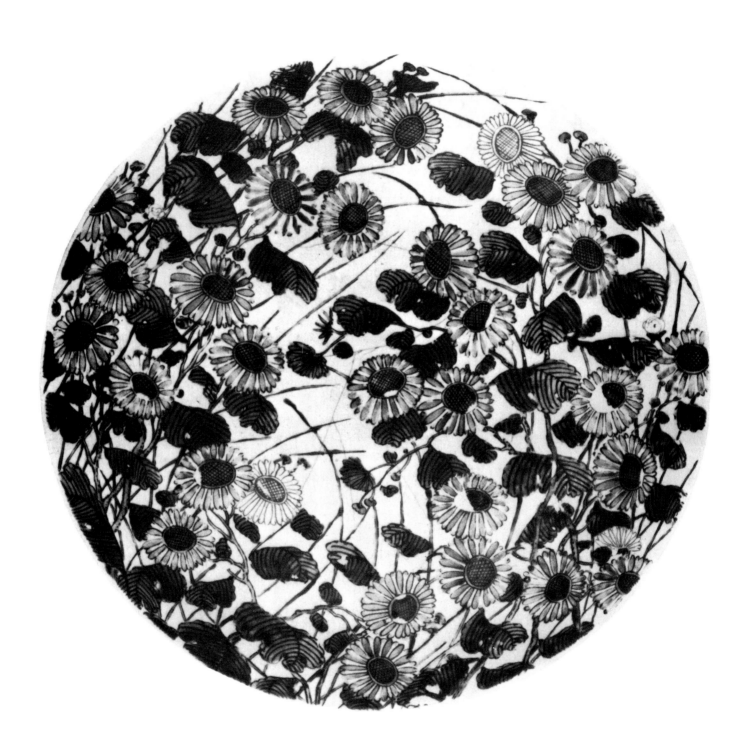

54 Kakiemon than Imari wares, so called after one of the ports of exportation. These generally entirely lack the subtlety found on Kakiemon ware. The artists who decorated Imari wares used the available space to the full; the designs in rather inky underglaze blue were completed with rich enamelled and gilded ornamentation which found favour with the Dutch, to whom the ware was mainly exported. To them Imari porcelain represented value for money since it was much cheaper than Chinese porcelain, and in particular large sets of vases and jars and covers (*garniture de cheminée*) were much in demand. The 18th-century pieces are sometimes decorated with representations of European merchants and their ships, but the standard ornamentation is floral. The Chinese made their own copies of the ware, showing on the whole a little more restraint in their choice of

decoration. Both Kakiemon and Imari ware continued to be made throughout the 19th century. Now, having been out of fashion for some time, Imari ware is once more gaining in popularity.

In another part of Japan, on the island of Honshū a porcelain totally different in character was made. This is Kutani ware, which has always found much favour with the Japanese themselves. Chinese landscapes of the late Ming were a favourite subject – but always executed in typical bold Japanese style with enamels that match the decoration in strength and boldness. The enamel colours are green, purple, yellow-red and blue. Another typical decorative motif is a curious, often geometric pattern, said to be derived from textiles. It is not always easy to know where a given piece has been made since a large group of Kutani types was produced at the kilns at Arita.

Perhaps the most celebrated of all 18th-century Japanese porcelains is Nabeshima ware. Made near Arita from about 1722, these wares are said to have been produced exclusively for the Nabeshima, a local noble family. This beautifully refined porcelain was decorated with floral designs in underglaze blue, embellished with delicate enamelling. On a typical piece the decoration covers part of the obverse and continues over the edge on the reverse. The most common shape is a shallow dish standing on a rather high foot. Pieces solely decorated in underglaze blue also occur, and the drawing as well as the potting is always exquisite. If this ware really was made only for the nobility, it would explain the uniformly high standard maintained.

There have always been potters who continued to make tea ceremony and allied wares in their own style, unimpressed with luxurious porcelains. Perhaps the most famous of all these was Ninsei, who worked in Kyoto and died in the late 17th century. His pieces, made of mainly enamelled pottery, combine the Japanese fondness for 'natural' surfaces with a very high degree of artifice, often with stunning results. This tradition has continued to the present and has always been popular.

BRONZES

Bronze artefacts of China, Tibet, Korea and Thailand preserve a high plateau of craftmanship through many historical periods, and some examples, by virtue of their extreme antiquity, provide our only knowledge of earliest rituals and social practices. The objects range from small items appealing to the modest collector to major pieces, almost landmarks of world art, eagerly sought by the greatest museums.

Chinese Bronzes

Ritual vessels. The Bronze Age in China opens around 1600 BC and ends with the fall of the Chou dynasty in 221 BC. This period covers three phases: the Shang dynasty in what is now Honan (1600–1027 BC); the main Chou period until about 770 BC; and a confused period of states warring amongst themselves that lasted until the 3rd century BC. Antique bronzes from these periods include sacrificial ritual vessels, which first appeared in the Shang dynasty, the ritual vessels of the Chou dynasty, and chariot fittings, mirrors and belthooks, which began to be made in the period of the Warring States.

In oracle taking, and in sacrificial or funerary ceremonies, ritual vessels were used to serve and cook offerings of food and wine. Such vessels also had secular uses, as is evident from inscriptions on some of them. They were formally presented to meritorious subjects, and during the Chou dynasty such gifts were a necessary part of feudal rule. The vessels also served to record events or actions, such as the division of land, a marriage, or the starting of a journey. The shapes of these early ritual vessels were not only copied for use as altar pieces in Confucian and other temples, but were copied in other materials, such as porcelain, jade, lacquer and enamel during the Sung and later dynasties.

125–130 The ritual vessels are best divided into groups according to their supposed function. Thus as food containers there are those known as *tou* and *kuei*; as food cookers the *li*, *ting* and *hsien*; as vessels for ceremonial ablutions the *chien* and *p'an*; as water or wine containers the *yü*, *hu*, *lei* and *fang-i*; as wine goblets the *chia*, *chüeh* and *ku*; and as wine servers the *ho* and *kuang*. The names have various origins: some are those inscribed on vessels of the Shang period, some are Sung identifications (AD 960–1279) and a few have recently been established by convention. During the course of time some shapes disappeared, while others underwent stylistic changes. Such developments, taken with the facts known about the evolution of decoration, provide clues which help to date many objects.

Two of the most remarkable ritual vessels are the *ting* and the *fang-i*. The *ting* was used in Chinese ritual for more than 3,000 years. The earliest type of *ting*—literally 'tripod vessel'—of about 1500–1300 BC, has a deep bowl and three short legs, pointed and slightly splayed. The more common *ting* of later Shang times has 57 a round body and three column legs, a shape persisting into the 10th century BC. A third type, appearing between the 11th and mid 10th centuries, is rectangular with four legs. A fourth type, comprising a shallow hemispherical bowl with 'cabriole' legs, first appeared about 900 BC and acquired a lid around 600 BC. This type continued to be made until the beginning of the Han dynasty (late 3rd century BC).

The *fang-i*, or square sacrificial vessel, is usually described as a wine holder. Although its exact purpose is uncertain, its high quality of casting and fine ornament leave no doubt of its ritual importance. The example illustrated is a late Shang type; early examples have 72 straight sides leaning slightly outwards, while later types bulge in a shallow curve. Ornamental handles may be added at the narrower ends, and the roof-shaped lid may be surmounted by a knob repeating that shape.

Not surprisingly, the origin and meaning of the decorative iconography is unknown. The main characteristic of Chinese bronze decoration is the representation of the bodies of real or mythical animals whose individual elements may be distorted or replicated to produce motifs in an endless stock of linear complications, executed in two or three levels of relief. Such decorative styles have also survived in carved white pottery and carved and inlaid wood, ivory and bone. Recognisable animal motifs occurring in Shang art are the tiger, snake, elephant and cicada (a vertical cicada pattern is illustrated). 57

A dominant relief of considerable importance is the *t'ao-t'ieh*. Western writers have described it variously as 137 'the great mastiff of Tibet' and 'the horned lion-griffin of Persian art'. It is prevalent from at least the 16th century BC and continues throughout the course of Chinese art, appearing in all mediums and, however stylised, remaining recognisable. Behind its many forms, whether bovine or feline, lies a tiger-like monster and the face of an ox or ram. Elements of the full-face mask such as the horns may be designed to represent other animals. In the Sung dynasty, these animals were identified with the *k'uei*, a mythological creature.

The earliest bronze vessels dating to the 15th century BC are decorated with figured bands in sharp relief on the shoulders and sides, in the middle of which the *t'ao-t'ieh* is repeated at least twice. However, the main trend after 1300 BC was to increase the decorated area so that it covered the whole surface. To do this, the mask was elaborated, expanded and sometimes dismembered, while the interstices were filled with spirals, which the

58 Tripod incense burner decorated with an inlaid design of metal foil. Sung dynasty, 960–1279.

72 Chinese called the 'thunder pattern'. This can be observed on the *fang-i*. The *k'uei* dragons could now be used separately from the mask and proved convenient for filling the narrower decorative bands at the neck or foot of a vessel.

A further line of development, from the mid 10th to mid 7th centuries BC, is characterised by patterned and grooved bands often based on a highly stylised bird design with elaborate tail and crest. This appears on *ting* throughout the 10th century. By the beginning of the

Chou dynasty the dragons and birds had become simple interlacing patterns which may cover the whole surface.

The period from the first quarter of the 5th century until the unification of the empire by the Ch'in emperor in 221 BC was characterised by a series of shifting alliances centred on the state of Ch'in in the west and Ch'u in the south. It was a time of rapid advance in iron metallurgy and bronze casting. Bronze vessels, weapons and ornaments excavated from tombs in the Huai river valley, an area annexed by the Ch'u state in the early 5th

59 An enlarged relief inscription from the base of the incense burner (58), reading 'Made by Hu Wên-ming of Yün-chien'. Victoria and Albert Museum, London.

60 Chariot axle caps with design of feathers and masks. 4th century BC. Victoria and Albert Museum, London.

century, followed the northern trend of small continuous patterns for decoration. They had one special feature – known as 'hook and volute' – which is best described as a triangular hook with a tight curl at the end. In the 4th century this motif was also adopted by jade carvers.

Other motifs generally known as Huai style, but also occurring in northern work, include rope and plait patterns, and the use of granulation, circles and parallel strokes on animals' bodies. Blade-shaped figures, whorls, scaled snakes and serpentine dragons as well as the familiar *t'ao-t'ieh* as an integral mask – all were elements in the Huai style, which lasted into the 4th century, when the motifs were gradually replaced by more geometric ones. Nevertheless, rectilinear ornament can appear on the same piece with scrolling figures reminiscent of animals, the pattern often being enhanced by gold or silver inlay work; this type represents the best metalwork of the 3rd century BC.

During the 2nd and 1st centuries BC inlay was gradually abandoned. The only traditional motif retained on bronze vessels of the Han dynasty was the full-face *t'ao-t'ieh* in the Huai style, which in the case of *hu* vessels was the only surface decoration. The gilding of vessels was introduced in the early Han dynasty; both gilding and inlay are found in a readily collectable form in belthooks (see page 64).

A scholarly antiquarian interest in early ritual vessels developed during the Sung dynasty (AD 960–1279) and led to the production of a class of bronzes which continued throughout the Yüan, Ming and Ch'ing dynasties. They were often of fine quality and reflected a new appreciation of the properties of bronze and experiments with its surface appearance. Shapes, ornament and inscriptions were investigated, and illustrated albums of bronzes began to appear in print at the end of the 11th century. It was probably this interest that prompted the manufacture of imitations of ancient vessels for several centuries afterwards. Of the four dynasties during which these bronzes were manufactured, the two earlier, Sung and Yüan, may be distinguished from the Ming and Ch'ing by the ingredients of the bronze alloy.

The most striking example of these late archaistic bronzes are the inlaid wares of the Sung dynasty and the bronzes of the Hsüan-tê reign (1426–35) during the Ming period. The Sung wares appear to have been modelled on inlaid ornaments of the 4th and 3rd centuries BC, though Sung craftsmen occasionally produced their own variations of gold and silver scrolling and interlacing. Many Hsüan-tê bronzes bear the emperor's reign mark but display new shapes and further surface variegations. Just as imperial blue and white porcelain of this reign period was much copied in later times, so too were many of these so-called 'palace bronzes'. Dating is thus problematical. Of all the bronze shapes, incense burners closely allied to Sung porcelain shapes appear to

58

61 Chariot rattle, the spherical part enclosing a small bronze ball. Warring States period, 4th or 3rd century BC.

Wên-ming, whose work, though in the Hsüan-tê style, 73 was in fact done in the late 16th and early 17th centuries. His signature includes the name of a renowed metal- 59 working centre in Kiangsu, and his work is remarkable for its finely cast relief and parcel gilding.

Ornamental bronzes: chariot fittings. A lesser activity, but one of comparable artistic distinction, was the manufacture and embellishment of bronze chariot fittings, which probably began during the Shang period. There was a wide variety of fittings, including axle caps, cross- 60,61 bar finials, pole shoes and heads, rail frontals and terminals, yoke knobs and forks, plaques and connections. Most of those made in the early part of the Chou dynasty (1027–249 BC) were decorated with typical Shang motifs—the *k'uei* dragon, the *t'ao-t'ieh* mask, the cicada, etc. The horses' bridles would be embellished with cowries and bronze buttons. Crossbars were decorated with four rattles, one over each yoke fork. Animal masks, such as the *t'ao-t'ieh*, were placed over the horses' foreheads. The need for axles to be protected was responsible for a continuous development in the design of axle caps. In the Western Chou period (1027–770 BC) they were shorter and stouter, often with an ornamental subdivision of ridges and grooves, or else a collar rim. Decorative patterns often consisted of scales and curves, those in Shang style being closed at the outer end, those in later Chou times appearing open like a short tube. 60

Funeral cortèges, particularly during the period 770– 475 BC, were the occasion for impressive displays of chariot bronze artistry. In some cases entire chariots were placed in the tombs, in others just the bronze fittings. Such is the wealth of fittings preserved from the later Warring States period (475–221 BC) that examples 62 have found their way into most of the world's museums and collections. They bear witness to the sophistication of metalworking and ornamentation of the period. Some are decorated in intricate patterns of gold and silver, inlaid with precious stones and glass, or even ornamented with animals in the round.

Ornamental bronzes: belthooks. In excellence of ornamental work no metal articles in ancient China were more prominent than belthooks. This group of objects 76 includes items that were clearly used as belthooks, and also others that may have been used to fasten dresses or tunics, or for pendants. Their size varies from 3–4 cm. to 15–20 cm. The earliest example known is dated to the 7th century BC, and by the Warring States period they had become a common article of dress. They carry elaborate designs with silver, gold, glass, turquoise and jade decoration. Some are entirely made of gold, others are carved from jade or ivory. Each is a unique creation.

The manufacture of belthooks required considerable

have been most numerous, and are reputed to have varied from deep yellow to dark purplish red in their surface colouring.

Also of interest are bronzes which ostensibly belong to the Chêng-tê reign (1506–21) and which have Arabic inscriptions, showing the Chinese interest in Islam. The Chêng-tê reign mark may be found on these bronzes, but it is no guarantee that they belong to that period. Mention should be made of one particular craftsman, Hu

technical competence in lapidary and metalwork. The bronze base was inlaid, often with beaten silver or gold foil; the use of foil permitted a single line to be of varying thicknesses, giving rise to an interplay of thick angular lines, curved lines, and fine spirals. Turquoise and malachite inlays are occasionally encountered, and in the 4th century BC copper was used to exploit the contrast between its red and the yellower colour of the bronze base.

In earlier Han times gilding was used on ornamental bronzes, and on belthooks it was especially successful. The gilding of some 4th- and 3rd-century BC specimens with Huai style ornament appears to have been only partly successful. But in larger examples of the 3rd and 2nd centuries a superior quality of burnished gilding is common, particularly on belthooks decorated in the 'chip carved' style, which date to the early Han period and copy a style of woodcarving.

Ornamental bronzes: mirrors. To some collectors Chinese mirrors form one of the most fascinating classes of early bronzes. The ornamentation is not only admirable in itself but also comprises mythical and cosmological symbols, mostly still a mystery.

Chinese bronze mirrors are thin discs highly polished on the reflecting side and decorated on the back with cast ornament in low relief. An essential feature of the design is the cast loop through which a cord could be passed for holding or suspending the mirror from the belt.

Mirrors are datable, and comparatively easily grouped, by their ornament, even though in the early period the patterns used were not necessarily similar to those on contemporaneous bronze vessels. In the Han period the ornament is a useful source of information about cosmological beliefs; moreover, in later Han times inscriptions alluded to mythological themes, and even to the manufacturing process. For purpose of identification and discussion mirrors are generally grouped according to their place of origin, for example Shou-hsien, Loyang; by motif, TLV, geometric, animal-zone, etc.; by period (Wang Mang, T'ang); or by school of thought, such as Taoist.

The earliest mirrors surviving in any number are probably of the 6th century BC. They often have a broad flat rim, and are decorated with four dragons in high relief, or a dragon band on a background of coarse 'thunder pattern'. Between the 5th and 3rd centuries a type appeared in southern China, in the Huai valley, which shares elements of decoration with contemporary bronze vessels, particularly the hook and volute pattern. A distinctive type of the Shou-hsien mirror is that bearing the *shan* ('mountain') ideograph. Those with hook and volute grounds may carry superimposed birds, dragons, bears or monkeys, usually in fours. By

contrast, in the north around Loyang, mirror ornament was dominated by lively dragon (or dragon-derived) figures against a background of lines and dots in low relief. These ceased to appear before the Han period.

Perhaps the most interesting decoration on Han mirrors – and certainly the most baffling – is the cosmological theme. A fundamental recurring device is the TLV pattern, or marks of that appearance, at fixed positions around the mirror. This is coupled with the animals of the Four Quarters (bird, tiger, dragon, tortoise with snake), and often other animals too, all depicted in swirling movement amid scrolling clouds. The elaborate TLV mirrors date to the reign of Wang Mang (AD 9–23). Many have inscriptions praising the metal, referring to the submission of 'the Barbarians', or describing the life of Taoist immortals. Characteristic Wang Mang mirrors have four pairs of bosses in the main field, an inscription surrounding the central ornament, and often a cloud pattern perhaps with swirling animals and human figures. The twelve mansions of the zodiac are represented by bosses and identified by Chinese characters naming them.

By contrast, many mirrors of the Han period have austere geometric designs, possibly of astrological

63 Porcelain prunus blossom vase, *mei-p'ing*, covered with a *sang de boeuf* ('ox blood') glaze. Lang ware of the K'ang-hsi period.

significance. They often feature star-shaped figures of eight points, twelve bosses as on TLV mirrors, or a concentric band and inscription referring to the brightness of the mirror, hence the classification 'Brilliance Mirrors'. A further type, the design of which persisted from the 1st century BC until the T'ang dynasty, is the animal-zone group. These portray realistic dragons and other celestial animals, have heavy rims, a central quatrefoil, and four, eight or seven bosses. Prescribed animal sequences appear, for example two birds, tiger, deer, tortoise with snake, dragon, feathered man. Conversely, mirrors featuring supposedly immortal human figures belong to the Taoist group. Other pieces in this group are characterised by a band of squares, each with 70

64 *left to right* Mei-p'ing with 'sacrificial red' glaze; 18th century. Bowl of ogee form with 'café au lait' glaze; mark and period of Ch'ien-lung. Bowl with incised dragons under a deep blue glaze; mid 17th century. Miniature vase with a 'tea dust' glaze; 18th or 19th century. Bottle with 'mirror black' glaze; K'ang-hsi period. Victoria and Albert Museum, London.

a four-character inscription and containing the Lord King of the East, the Queen Mother of the West and other deities, together with horned and winged dragons, or tigers.

The range of mirrors in later periods varies; for example few Sung mirrors are known. After those of the third century AD it is T'ang mirrors that deserve most attention. They display a high quality of metalwork and craftsmanship and occur not only in plain bronze but also decorated with gold and silver. Thin sheets of gold or silver foil would be attached to the back with chased, traced or openwork ornament, often on a punched ground, and executed in finer detail than was possible in bronze. Some pieces have small floral or figural motifs

cut from foil and laid in a lacquer surface. Lotus petal rims, and decorations of scrolling floral designs with 71 birds, vines and grapes, were fashionable, as also was the 74 phoenix, the mythological successor of the 'Red Bird of the South', and the lion, a Buddhist symbol.

Buddhist Bronzes

The arrival of Buddhism in China in the 2nd century AD gave the bronze caster new themes for his craft. From at least the 4th to the 10th centuries small gilt bronze Buddhas and figures from the Buddhist pantheon were made as travelling icons or for small altars. The figures were small in scale, were cast from base metals and were gilded by an application of gold leaf to the surface, aided by mercury. Occasionally the base, a trapezium stand on four legs, would bear a dated inscription.

The inscriptions describe the occasion for which the object was fashioned, the name of the donor and the cyclical year in which it was made. However, false

66 'TLV' mirror, so called because of the occurrence of the mysterious signs reminiscent of those letter-shapes in the decoration. Note also the swirling band of celestial animals. 1st century BC–1st century AD.

attributions or inscriptions have in some cases been added later. Today the largest collections of Chinese Buddhist bronzes are in the United States, particularly in the Fogg Art Museum and the Metropolitan Museum. Some examples still appear on the market, their price varying according to age and quality, whether they are dated or not, and the degree of aesthetic or iconographic interest they may have. Some images may in fact be modern casts made from a mould that has itself been taken from a genuinely old specimen; only a close examination of the carving and patina can reveal their newness. Completely modern forgeries may be exposed by poor workmanship or faulty iconography, for stylistic and iconographical combinations are likely to occur that were never represented in genuine images. Most modern forgeries are small in size.

The iconography of Buddhist bronzes is complex. The various poses and hand gestures represent different attitudes of meditation and teaching. There are Buddhas and Bodhisattvas, the former always simple and 132,133

67 *left to right* Bowl and cover with decoration of dragons. Small wine cup with lotus flowers. Saucer dish with mandarin ducks in a lotus pond, the border with Sanskrit script. All three pieces are enamelled in *tou-ts'ai* style and belong to the Yung-chêng period.

68 Pair of small bowls with five-clawed dragons chasing 'flaming pearls' in green on a yellow ground. Mark and period of Ch'ien-lung.

69 *Famille rose* decorated bowl and wine cup with saucer. Yung-chêng or Ch'ien-lung period. Victoria and Albert Museum, London.

70 Mirror showing elements of Taoist folk-lore. Four Taoist deities and four dragons with monster heads are separated by eight bosses in the central band; the rim is cast with a band of running dragons and phoenix. 2nd or 3rd century AD.

unadorned, the latter richly attired and attended by certain objects such as a vase, a scroll or an animal. Minor deities are also portrayed. The most important of these are the guardian deities, characterised by fierce muscular figures able to scare away evil demons.

The complex iconography of the pantheon is a matter for the specialist, and only a few characteristics can be mentioned here to show how most examples can be identified by their role in the pantheon and, possibly, their position in time. Thus we find one of the earliest bronze Buddha images, Śākyamuni, seated on a lion throne, hands in meditation pose and clad in monk's robes. Another image, of the late 5th century, shows the Buddha in a garment that leaves the shoulder bare; the Buddha holds the hem. Another Buddha of the period stands on a lotus base and wears a monk's habit. The Maitreya Buddha of the 6th century is portrayed standing with legs slightly apart on a lotus base with a smile on his lips and wearing characteristic winged robes. Images of the T'ang period are more sensuous, with more

75

rounded face and body features. The medicine Buddha, Yao Shih Fo, carries a medicine jar and golden fruit. Avalokiteśvara, known in Chinese as Kuan-yin and especially familiar in porcelain, is usually identifiable by the ambrosia bottle or lotus flowers she holds; but a distinctive characteristic is a small Buddha figure set in the front of the crown. Manjusri, the Bodhisattva of Wisdom, is often shown riding a lion, while Sāmanta-bhadra, the Bodhisattva of Universal Benevolence, normally rides an elephant.

Thai Buddhas

The Buddhist art of Thailand essentially reflects regional styles and thus the historical political dominance whose centres shifted so frequently in the Indochinese peninsula. Little is known of artistic development in Thailand until the establishment of the Mon Dvāravatī kingdom (6th–11th centuries AD). This period coincided with control of the Malay peninsula by the Śrīvijaya empire of Sumatra, but in the 11th century the Khmer kingdom annexed central Thailand and part of the Malay penin-

72 Ritual vessel, *fang-i*, wine container, decorated with a *t'ao-t'ieh* against a spiral 'thunder pattern' background, the footrim with a band of *k'uei* dragons. Shang dynasty, 12th or 11th century BC.

73 Incense burner by Hu Wên-ming with relief design of fabulous animals among waves and above them a band of Taoist emblems. 17th century.

74 Mirror of silvered bronze with two phoenix, a crane in flight and a mandarin duck on a lotus flower. Flowers and bees decorate the rim. T'ang dynasty, 618–906.

75 Chinese gilt bronze figure of the Maitreya Buddha with flame-shaped nimbus, standing on a lotus throne. The winged projections at the hem of his robe are characteristic of the period, and the pedestal bears an inscription (not visible in the illustration) with a date corresponding to AD 536. University Museum, Philadelphia.

sula. By the 13th century the Thai people had established their own kingdom of Sukhodaya in central Thailand.

All these states developed their own traditions of Buddhist art. Bronze Buddhas in the Dvāravatī style are generally small statuettes made of solid metal without a core. The bronze artefacts of the Śrīvijaya kingdom are of a copper alloy containing no tin, suggesting a Sumatran origin. They are often elaborately decorated versions of the Bodhisattva Avalokiteśvara. During the period 1000–c.1220 AD when the Khmers of Cambodia dominated central Thailand with their capital at Lopburî, a regional style of Khmer art known as Khmer-Lopburî was produced. It reflects the Khmer fusion of Hinduism and Buddhism and ancestor worship, the sculptures combining human portraiture and divine images. The faces are square with sharply delineated lips and eyebrows. Many were made for household as well as ceremonial use.

Under the Sukhodaya kingdom, which by the end of the 13th century had superseded the Khmers, there

76 Ornamental bronze work. *a, b, f* are all decorative fittings for weapons of the Warring States period (4th–3rd centuries BC), inlaid with gold and silver. The belthooks are *c, d, e. c* is a tiger in gilt bronze entwined with two snakes and with turquoise inlay; *d* is inlaid with gold wire and turquoise on three facets and has an animal-head hook; *e* shows a fine use of wire inlay and turquoise. Warring States period.

77 Korean bronze *kundika*, Buddhist water sprinkler, covered with a green patination. Koryŏ period, 932–1392.

a

b

c

d

e

f

78 Thai Buddha seated on a lotus throne, his hands in *bhūmisparśa mudra*. Chieng Sèn style. About 15th century.

79 Thai Buddha of the Û Tòng style. 13th or 14th century. Musée Guimet, Paris.

was a change of emphasis. Bronzes combined conventions taken from both Khmer and Burmese styles. Long oval faces with full cheeks and fine regular features, finely bridged and slightly hooked noses, high-arched eyebrows, downcast eyes, the hair in tight formalised curls reaching a point above the forehead and surmounted by a flame, symbol of spiritual fire: all these shaped the ideal, even into the 20th century.

In northern Thailand during the 13th to 16th centuries, the state of Lân Nâ flourished independently of the Sukhodaya kingdom. Its capital was Chieng Sèn, and a large range of northern Thai Buddhist art is known as Chieng Sèn style. However, it is probably more accurate to classify the thousands of extant examples representing the northern style as belonging to the Chieng Mai type of the 14th century, Chieng Mai being the northern capital after 1296.

Another distinct stylistic group takes its name from the region of Û Tòng in the south, where a separate group of Thais established a kingdom about the middle of the 14th century. A large number of bronze images were produced in this area; Ayudhyā was the main centre, though some Û Tòng bronzes were made in Cambodia and Sukhodaya. They are generally remarkable for their

signed works were produced during the last years of the Lamaistic period, at the external centre of Peking. The Chinese were heavily involved in Tibetan political affairs from 1705 until the end of the 19th century. Lamaism was encouraged in China, particularly under the Yung-chêng emperor and his successor Ch'ien-lung, who is reputed to have given his mother several pantheons of Tibetan deities.

Tantric Buddhism comprises a complex mixture of beliefs based on Tantras, or manuals, which prescribe paths of mystical practices. Nevertheless, familiar figures appear in its pantheon – the historical Buddha (Śākyamuni), the Buddha of the future (Maitreya), the meditative Buddhas and the eight great Bodhisattvas, now accompanied by female beings, the Tārās. These figures may stand alone or be grouped precisely in systems known as *mandalas*, which are based on the cosmos. A *mandala* is likely to consist of several divine figures surrounding a central figure, which in turn is part of a higher-placed figure, the whole being absorbed in a single central high figure. Such groups are occasionally united in a composite figure with numerous hands, arms and heads. The highest union is represented by the divine figure coupled with its female complement, Sakti.

The Tantric system also includes highly placed divine figures who have the appearance of demons and are commonly known as protectors of the sacred teaching. Such a figure can be recognised by its heavy build and rigid bearing, glaring eyes, bushy eyebrows, thick nose, gaping jaws and flowing hair.

By contrast with Chinese work, Tibetan bronzes may be finished by painting the face, eyes, hair, palms and soles, usually in bright colours. The Bodhisattvas and Tārās clothed in rich Indian attire may be decorated with inlays of small coloured stones such as turquoise or coral, or in later works with coloured glass. Occasionally the base of a work may bear the name of the deity or its place of origin in Tibetan, Nepalese or Chinese script, but more often just the sacred symbol of the thunderbolt. The base plate closes off the hollow inside the figure, which was originally intended to hold *mantras*, that is, prayers and other relics.

A Buddhist bronze form which deserves mention by reason of its prevalence is the water sprinkler, or *kundika*, of which a Korean example is discussed here. Used as a Buddhist ritual vessel, it is a shape produced both in bronze and ceramic and is known throughout much of the Buddhist world. One of the finest examples, dated to the Koryō period (AD 936–1392), belonging to the National Museum of Korea, is decorated with inlaid silver and has a design of willows, ducks and water, effectively offset by a fine patina, a characteristic of many of these bronze forms.

severe soldierly dignity and square Khmer-looking jaws.

Tibetan Buddhas

A difficulty in discussing Tibetan art objects is that their origin and age are not easily determined. Moreover, what Western scholars group under the collective term 'Tibetan' comprises work from western China as well as the southern frontier areas, Nepal, Sikkim and Bhutan. Tibetan art is interwoven with a form of Tantric Buddhism known as Lamaism and as such primarily serves a ritual purpose. In view of this, standards of art, precise geographical origin and even age have to be a secondary consideration.

Generally speaking, few works that can be dated earlier than the 17th century are known in Western collections. Apart from comparisons with dated examples, almost the only guide to dating is the rough and ready one of attributing works of superior craftsmanship and higher standard of materials to the earlier period. The artist is normally anonymous, but some

JADE AND HARDSTONES

Chinese Jade

Chinese jade is probably best-known in the West in the form of bright green jewellery, picturesquely called 'kingfisher jade'. However, a wealth of jade work exists, the earliest of which antedates this jewellery jade by more than 3,000 years; and it includes shapes of the utmost intricacy and colours of many varieties.

The term 'jade' denotes two very similar stones, nephrite and jadeite, which were worked into implements by neolithic man. The best-known finds have been in Switzerland, western France and China, but others have been reported in many parts of Europe, Asia and America. When the stone cultures were succeeded by bronze and iron users, jade lost its value as a tool, and as a gem-stone, in all but a few regions.

Early Spanish navigators to Mexico and Central America brought the first carved jades to Europe. They were worn in the New World as ornaments, amulets and badges of rank, though for the Spaniards they were associated with a cure for a disease of the kidneys. The Spanish term *'piedra-de-ijada'*, 'stone of the loins', was the source of the English word 'jade'. This Aztec and Mayan jade was in fact jadeite.

Neither nephrite nor jadeite is indigenous to China; the Chinese imported it from Khotan and Chinese Turkestan. Nephrite is known in China as 'true jade', and it has been worked there from the earliest times to the present. Although white in its pure form, with chemical impurities it takes on a range of colours, the best-known among collectors being 'spinach' green. It is cold to the touch and does not warm in the hand. It cannot be scratched by steel. What is known in the West as jade is usually the translucent green stone jadeite, worked in China only during the last two hundred years.

Both substances are hard and have to be worked with abrasives such as quartz sand, powdered garnets or corundum. They differ in physical properties. The fibres of nephrite are rarely visible to the naked eye. Jadeite may be granular or fibrous, but more commonly the former; individual grains can be seen in thin, translucent bowls. Both are tough but brittle. The green of nephrite is due to the presence of iron, whereas in jadeite the source is chromium. The range of nephrite colours is greater, comprising white, grey-white, 'mutton fat' or yellow-white and yellow, pale green, moss green, spinach green, brown, rust-brown and black. Jadeite may be snow white, emerald green, lavender blue, or mixtures of all three. 'Kingfisher jade' is Burmese jadeite. The term 'imperial jade' was originally applied to jade from palace collections, but is now used more widely for commercial purposes.

Neolithic carvings in jade fall into two groups; ornamental amulets or pendants, and ceremonial or ritual objects. With few exceptions the ceremonial objects are flat slabs not more than a few millimetres thick; they are thought to have been symbols of power or rank. They include thin plaques called *kuei* (see line drawing). 138 Some appear to be instruments, their forms derived from other tools, such as the dagger, hand adze, and bronze-socketed spear-head. They also include the so-called annular disc *pi*, called the 'Symbol of Heaven', and tubes 83 with square outer and round inner perimeters, called *tsung* (see line drawing), whose purpose is still obscure. 131

Even after the working of bronze became widespread, it appears that bamboo drills were still used to cut circular channels, such as that in the *pi*, though bronze tools with abrasives gave greater precision. There is no evidence for the use of a rotary tool on early jades except for the making of perforations.

83 Jade ritual disc, *pi*, called 'Symbol of Heaven'. It is a pale green with darker markings. Neolithic style, Shang – mid Chou dynasties.

84 Jade figure of a camel. Sung dynasty, 960–1279 or earlier. Victoria and Albert Museum, London.

During the Shang and early Chou dynasties (*c.* 1600–771 BC) there appears to have been a considerable production of carvings in animal form. They are stylised and abstract, and are not rounded figures but thin plaques in animal form. They are basically feline, bovine or fish-shaped and show no trace of primary cutting, the edges being accurately ground to right angles. A notable feature is the hole near the top of these figures, suggesting that they were used as amulets. By comparison with the iconography of contemporary bronzes, many may be dated to the Shang or early Chou dynasties.

The advent of the Iron Age around 500 BC led to further developments in jade carving. The 5th to 3rd centuries saw the flowering of philosophical schools, and

85

85 Small jade ornamental plaques of the Shang and Chou dynasties; *top right* is a dragon plaque from a girdle pendant of the Warring States period, 5th–3rd centuries BC.

86 Jade group of two puppies with curled tails; the jade is pale yellowish green with light brown markings. Perhaps Six Dynasties, 3rd–6th centuries AD.

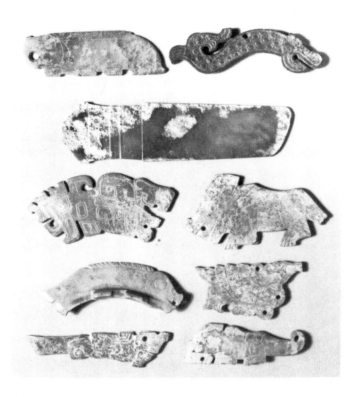

there may have been 'schools' engaged in the making of particular classes of objects. The *kuei* and *pi* of conventional form but with 'grain pattern' surface decoration must have been in great demand. In burials of the Warring States period *pi* are found at either side of the head and under the knees.

Ornamental plaques of complex openwork design also belong to this period. They are shaped as intertwined serpentine monsters, sometimes linked with other monsters, and suggestive of the bronze motifs cast in the same period. They are presumed to have been used as girdle pendants, perhaps by court officials, as the

ingenuity of their design and skill with which they were executed make them outstanding within the jade carving tradition. During the early Han dynasty (206 BC–AD 220) girdle pendants were replaced by belthooks and beltrings of jade or metal, or both. At this period jade was also used for sword and scabbard furniture.

From the 3rd century AD onwards the dating of jade is problematical. Excavations in which jade objects are found are of limited help, since the objects may have been treasured possessions of an earlier date than that of their burial. Sometimes analogies can be drawn with the style and subject of pottery vessels and figurines recovered from Han and T'ang graves. Such are the small animal carvings. However, colour, finish, quality and execution – and scientific analysis – are more consistent guides to dating.

Small animal carvings are compact and simple but reveal aptly the animal portrayed. A greyhound is carved with ribcage showing, ears back, and seated – but flexed with alertness. Sometimes striated colours in the stones or the shape itself are used to the carver's advantage. The camel with its head turned back is reminiscent of the pebble shape, the pony knapping its hind hoof and the mandarin duck with head among its back feathers follow the same patterns.

Some jade vessels appear to have been influenced by ancient ritual vessels, and some of these jades may be tentatively dated to the Sung dynasty. They are, much simplified in form, cups and libation vessels whose decoration of stylised monster masks, modelled spirals, climbing dragons, or the thunder pattern border are all motifs familiar in bronze. Certain large animal carvings, notably of horses and water buffaloes, are normally attributed to the Ming dynasty, but a later date cannot be ruled out. They are large (for example 25 cm.), with simple but careful carving, done in grey, black, spinach green, brown, pale celadon or white nephrite.

By contrast many jade carvings of high quality and excellent design were executed in the Ch'ing period, especially during the reign of Ch'ien-lung (1736–95). Thousands were added to the imperial collections, some of them inscribed with poems in the imperial calligraphy. Among new uses found for jade were jade-handled brushes, seals, arm-rests, brushpots, cosmetic boxes and teapots. These reflected the fact that greater quantities of nephrite were entering China than ever before. Certain choice colours and textures, such as 'mutton fat', were highly prized. Nevertheless, it is the larger works, such as incense burners and vases, modelled after ancient bronze forms and characterised by loose ring handles and chains, for which the Ch'ing dynasty, and the period from the beginning of Ch'ien-lung's reign, were renowned.

88 Pale green jade vase and cover with ring handles. 18th century. Victoria and Albert Museum, London.

89 *left* A malachite carving in simple lotus leaf form. *right* A lotus leaf in chalcedony with small white flower and a climbing snail. 18th or 19th century.

90 Jade boulder carving showing five scholars looking at a scroll which bears the circular *yin-yang* symbol. 18th century.

91 Sword handle in jade with inlay of rubies and gold. Mogul style. Victoria and Albert Museum, London.

92 White jade bowl, the shallow carved design of a fish, probably a carp, symbolising achievement in the official examinations. 18th or 19th century.

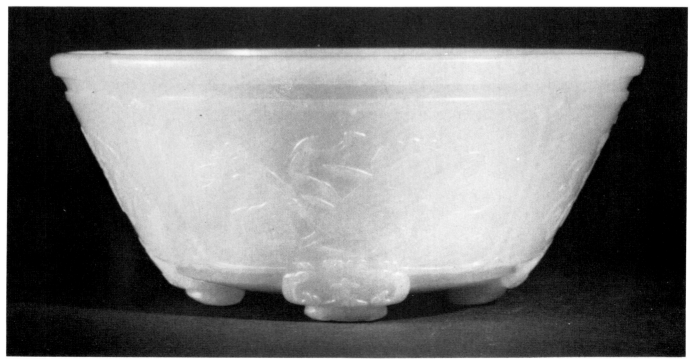

93 Rock crystal vase embellished with gnarled branches and a green bird. 18th or 19th century.

94 Pale green jade bowl in Mogul style.

Numerous pictorial carvings now appeared, and some were duplicated in hardstone. Representatives of the 90 type are boulder carvings, with mountainous landscapes, rocks and pines, hidden paths and pavilions, and perhaps a wandering scholar. In contrast to the rococo-type 92 incense burners, vessels with very simple contours were produced throughout the Ch'ing period: round shapes, shapes with straight sides of smooth lines, or shapes based on highly conventionalised flower forms. The thinness obtained in the vessel walls indicates the high quality of the craftsmanship.

Jade carving in nephrite and jadeite has been carried out with great skill in the present century, especially in Peking. Snuff bottles, plain bowls, pendants and other carvings, as well as antique shapes, are all in the repertoire of the modern carver. In recent decades the use of fine grade carborundum has given modern jade a brilliant finish rarely attainable in ancient times.

Indian Jade

A tradition of jade carving also existed in India, though it lasted for less than four hundred years, flourishing

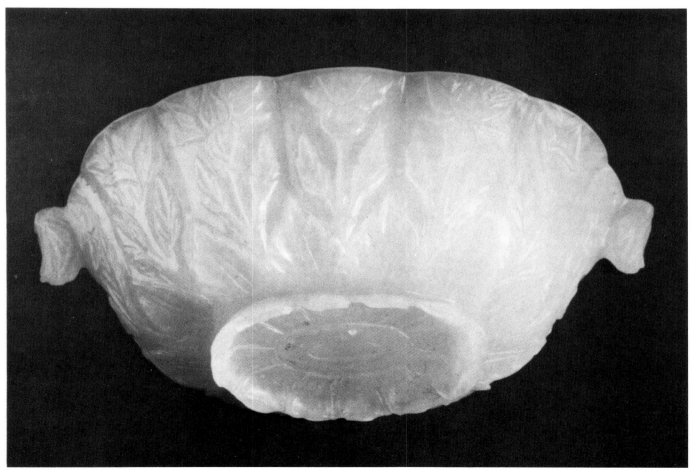

95 Soapstone standing figure of the Taoist immortal, Chung-li Ch'üan, with his fan; the figure is predominantly russet coloured but with yellowish face. 17th or 18th century.

during the 17th century, under the Moguls. Large nephrite vessels were made, often of lobed form, influenced by gourds, lotus leaves or petals. Animal motifs reflected Persian and Mongol influence (the horse and the ibex), and the vessels were sometimes ornamented with gold and precious stones, especially rubies, sapphires and emeralds. Sometimes the carving is done in such minute detail that overlapping lotus petals on 94 the vessel wall are themselves carved with a floral design. Sword handles of light green nephrite are also 91 inlaid or incised with floral designs, sometimes encrusted with sapphires, diamonds, rubies and emeralds in gold settings. Flower designs incorporate numerous spiked petals, as well as the lotus; a lotus bud often forms the knob for the lid of a bowl or ewer.

Chinese Hardstones

The term 'hardstone' covers such widely differing materials as amber, a kind of resin; jet, a type of fossilised coal; coral, the deposit of a sea creature; and even rhinoceros horn. It also includes several groups of stones, the largest being quartz, to which chalcedony in all its forms belongs.

The working of hardstone, like that of jade, involves the use of sharp stone or metal points or wheels in combination with abrasive materials. A characteristic of Oriental, and particularly Chinese, hardstone carving is the care taken to preserve the nature of the stone by making full use of its colours. This may be seen in the white flower nestling in the corner of a blue chalcedony 89 leaf, or in the green bird on the rock crystal vase. Even 93 the face of a figure may be picked out in pale soapstone, 95 while the robes fit into the red or dark colour of the stone. This medium was one of the richest sources of illustrations of Chinese folk-lore, myths and legends.

96 Soapstone seated figure of Pu-tai, the laughing Buddha, his arm resting on his money bag. 17th or 18th century.

97 Chinese cloisonné enamel tripod incense burner with champlevé handles and decorated with lotus scrolls, the small 'arrow vase' similarly decorated. First half of the 15th century.

The quartz family has been used for jewellery and carved objects all over the world. In its many forms the stone is fairly hard and has a glossy lustre which takes a high polish much sought by connoisseurs. Rock crystal, colder than glass and so called because of its icy clarity, is a crystallised variety of quartz. In China it was used for such objects as large animal carvings and figures of the Buddha, as well as ornamental vessels often embellished **93** in high relief with trailing plants and other foliage. The crystal may contain gas, water or liquid that moves as the piece is moved, or crystals of other minerals, giving rise to colour or cloud effects.

Chalcedony includes cornelian and agate, and also therefore onyx, which is a variety of agate. Common chalcedony occurs in a wide range of pale colours and was used for some of the most fascinating Chinese carvings of the 18th century, subtle in colours and subject matter; it even appears inconsequentially, as a snail on a leaf. However, the stone is very porous and can be artificially coloured.

Startling colours are provided by malachite, the green **89** of which indicates the presence of hydrated carbonate of copper. The surface is often marked with rings or layers of different shades of green or finely figured veins which are exploited to the full in one rendering of the lotus leaf, the craftsman adding a shallow stalk on the underside.

Lapis lazuli, a crystalline limestone that was imported from Tibet, was popular in the Ch'ien-lung period. Snuff bottles, seals, brush washers, miniature vases and small animal carvings were all made in this material. Turquoise was used as a decorative inlay, especially during the first millennium BC in bronzes of all kinds, and subse- **76** quently in jewellery and small carvings.

Of all hardstones, soapstone or steatite has been used to the greatest extent. It is a variety of talc, soft, smooth, soapy to the touch, superficially like marble, and sometimes mistaken for jade. So soft that it may be worked with a knife, it has provided some of the liveliest and most amusing of all hardstone carvings, and may be **96** found in many colours and colour combinations.

ENAMELS

The fascination of enamels lies in the appeal of the pure bright colours, and Chinese and Japanese work is certainly outstanding in its variety of colours and colour mixes. Cloisonné, champlevé, repoussé and painted enamels are among the techniques employed, but the basic enamelling process is the same. All require a glass paste or powder mixed with flux to promote melting, and a metallic oxide pigment which is applied to a metal base (bronze, copper, silver, gold). When fired at a sufficiently high temperature the paste melts and adheres to the metal. Subsequent stages vary according to the effect intended, but may include rubbing smooth and refiring, or filling surface pittings with coloured wax.

Enamel and metal is essentially a fragile combination, strain being placed on the fusion if the article is subjected to varying conditions of heat and cold. The difficulty of securing the enamel to its base can be reduced by breaking it up into small cells. In the cloisonné method the cells are divided by thin wires, in the champlevé method they are carved out of the solid metal base, and in the repoussé method they are hammered out of a metal sheet. The significance of Limoges in this connection was that it led in the technique of painting in enamel colours on a white background enamel that was already secured to its metal base by firing, and could be fired again to fix the painted decoration. In China work of this kind came to be known as Canton enamel.

Chinese Enamels

The earliest known enamels occur in Mycenaean jewellery attributed to the 13th century BC. The Chinese had the materials and techniques required for enamel work from the 5th century BC, but there is no evidence that it was carried out with any regularity until the 15th century AD, and no Chinese cloisonné work appears to have reached Europe before the 19th century. Chinese cloisonné is broadly datable to centuries rather than Chinese reigns. It can be analysed according to the development of its technique; by the introduction of new colours; or occasionally by vessel shapes which may correspond to shapes in contemporary lacquer and porcelain.

The period mark on an object, usually incised in the base, is not a reliable guide to dating, even when the date appears in enamel within the design itself. Fortunately the technical development of cloisonné work has several landmarks that help with dating. These include the composition of the base of the work and that of the wires, and the methods by which they were attached to the body.

The bases of the earliest 15th-century works are made of a cast copper alloy close to bronze. The wires are also made of this alloy and are hammered out of the metal ingot. This process gives them a tendency to split, and finished works with split wires may be broadly dated to before the second half of the 17th century. They were attached to the base by solder until about this time.

In the early 16th century the use of copper sheet for bases became current. These were hammered into shape and soldered together, and this method was employed from that time onwards, though there were exceptions. The wires which postdate the late 17th century are copper and were produced more easily by being drawn through a die, which also removed their tendency to split. Vegetable adhesive was also current after this date. This burnt up in the firing and left the wires supported directly by the enamel.

The background decoration, which is a functional necessity in securing the enamel to the base since wide unsupported areas of enamel are unstable, may also give some indication of the period of manufacture. In the early 15th century the design, usually floral scrolls, supplied the main theme and filled all the space available, every leaf and tendril playing its part in supporting the enamel. However, by the 16th century a secondary type of scroll work often bearing no relation to the main design came into use as a functional background filler.

The colours themselves vary most in cloisonné. Those of the first half of the 15th century are simple, usually a turquoise blue blackground and a scheme including dark green, sometimes almost black, as well as cobalt blue, red, yellow and white. In the second half of the century new colours were used including a semi-transparent purple, rather pale at first and known as 'Ming pink'. It consisted of large red and white fragments of colour which in firing joined but did not fuse. This was the only pink available until the early 18th century when a rose pink enamel was widely used. The first mixed colours are followed at the end of the 15th century by a paler green consisting of fragments of yellow and green, while in the early 16th century a turquoise green and semi-

99 Pair of Canton enamel dishes showing the design front and back.
18th century.

translucent brown made their appearance. By the middle of the 16th century complex mixed colours, using as many as three separate pastes for one colour, came into use. 17th-century colours were even more complex, but were simplified again towards the end of the period, perhaps as a result of imperial standardisation about 1680. Seen overall, it is the turquoise blue of Chinese cloisonné, especially of the 15th and 18th centuries, that is outstanding. The Japanese were unable to match it until the late 19th century.

Stylistically, the development of cloisonné work can be traced from the 15th century. Examples are not numerous, but those extant are in many respects close to contemporary porcelain and lacquer. The cloisonné wares are characterised by a good depth of enamel, cast bronze bases, skilfully placed fine wires, simple designs and clear striking colours. A prominent feature is the compact lotus scroll. A key colour apart from the turquoise blue is a lapis lazuli tinged with purple. Many 15th-century incense burners have handles decorated with champlevé. Some stylistically early pieces bear the mark of Hsüan-tê and can be regarded as being of that period.

The shapes of 15th-century cloisonné pieces indicate ceremonial rather than domestic use, in contrast to contemporary porcelain and lacquer. The almost exclusive employment of lotus scrolls for decoration suggests use in Buddhist temples. Shapes of particular interest include the secular cupstands, which have a counterpart in celadon and blue and white of the 14th and 15th centuries; beaker vases based on the archaic bronze *ku* form; the *kuei* incense burner; and the *kundika* or water sprinkler in regular use in Lamaistic ritual and produced in ceramic and bronze form in many parts of the Buddhist

world. Cast bronze boxes with decorations of grape vines, persimmon and pomegranates belong to the mid 15th century, followed later in the century by cloisonné ware resembling the porcelain *fa-hua* type so well known round 1600. A number of pieces bearing the 15th-century mark of the Ching-t'ai emperor can be found, but stylistic criteria suggest a true dating to the mid 17th century or later.

The 16th century is dominated by the long reigns of two emperors who were great patrons of the arts, Chia-ching (1522–66) and Wan-li (1573–1619). Porcelains, lacquer and textiles flourished, but not until the end of the 16th century did cloisonné figure strongly. Of shapes, the *ku* beaker-vase is commonly found, as is the *ting* (tripod incense burner), which was close to contemporary bronze forms. Bowls were common, often with Buddhist devices or emblems such as the lion and brocade ball, the lotus petal and the triangular border. Also dated to this period are slender ewers with flattened pear-shaped bodies and domed lids such as are found in contemporary blue and white porcelain.

Other wares were large dishes decorated with five-clawed dragons on a pale turquoise blue background, deep flat-based dishes decorated with landscapes, plants, animals, birds and human figures, and also dishes of cast bronze whose central decorative theme was set in a background differing in colour from the border. Here the subjects included cranes, water plants and mandarin ducks in a lotus pond. All these 16th-century pieces incorporated a new and more complex range of colours often numbering as many as eleven, and including the composite green-yellow and Ming pink.

The 17th century was a time of internal difficulties unresolved until the 1680s – in fact a time when official patronage of the arts almost disappeared. It was not until the end of the century that new cloisonné methods made an impact, becoming firmly established in the 18th century. Of the 17th-century pieces the most imposing are the huge vases, incense burners and candlesticks made in sets for Buddhist temples. Formal lotus scrolls or archaistic designs derived from ancient bronzes dominated the decoration, and the enamels cover a wide range of colours set against a deep turquoise ground. The four-sided jar based on the bronze *hu* shape is a good example of an early 17th-century type and exhibits the characteristic border of horses galloping over waves. Some jars of this type have less formal decoration – landscapes, rocks, animals and plants – but fully exploit the use of mixed colours.

A new factory for the manufacture of cloisonné enamels was set up in Peking around 1680, one of thirty under the patronage of the K'ang-hsi emperor. Both he and his successor, Yung-chêng, are believed to have commissioned large cloisonné vessels for temple use, as

their predecessors had done. Ritual vessels reputed to be over six feet high were provided for the great Lama monastery of Yung-ho-kung. Few pieces have come to light with the mark of K'ang-hsi and none with that of Yung-chêng. Thus it is difficult to identify positively any Ch'ing cloisonné as belonging to these two reigns, except insofar as it is known that copper wire instead of bronze was in general use by the Ch'ien-lung period, and that the striking rose-pink enamel derived from gold was in use after the first quarter of the 18th century.

By contrast, a wealth of material bears the marks of the Ch'ien-lung emperor, and their most striking feature is the brightness of their cobalt blue. Moreover they are in a better state of preservation than earlier works, the final wax application to the post-firing pittings having been carefully applied. Distinctive enamel colours include dark turquoise green, pale yellowish greens, purples and lilacs, and of course the rose pink, which is well represented in the plum-blossom of the box illustrated here. Prevalent shapes are small vases modelled after the bronze *hu*, tankards derived from a 15th-century blue and white porcelain type, and miniature sets of boxes, incense burners and small vases invariably decorated with formal lotus scrolls, some of these latter wares bearing the incised reign mark in four or six characters. Model animals and birds were also made in cloisonné; quails, cranes and ducks, and also miniature ponies and elephants, were popular. Many of the large cloisonné vessels such as incense burners of the Ch'ien-lung period were further enhanced with repoussé work.

The absence of pieces with marks later than the

98

101

Ch'ien-lung period means that 19th-century cloisonné has to be dated by analogy with contemporary porcelain. Scrolling designs may be slightly stiffer, more formal and more symmetrical than before, or there may be a preference for different background colours such as yellow.

Finally, there are some late 19th-century imitations of Ming dynasty bowls which use thinly applied enamels and inferior designs. However, a late date is indicated where no solder is found to have secured the wires. In some cases a bronze plaque on the base is inscribed with the words 'Ming copy' and carries a drawing of a conical hat with a tassel!

99 *Canton enamel.* One of the most attractive classes of enamel is known as painted enamel. Its smooth off-whites, gentle metallic colours and fragile appearance suggest porcelain rather than enamel work. True painted enamels were perfected in the 17th century in Europe and were the forerunners of Chinese 'Canton enamel'. The vogue in the West for Chinese porcelain in the 17th and 18th centuries extended to Canton enamel but ignored Chinese cloisonné. The process of painting enamel on copper seems to have arrived in China at about the same time as the rose pink enamel, responsible for the contemporary *famille rose* palette, appeared on porcelain. Both materials displayed the same subject matter: interior scenes with furniture, antiques and flower vases; or landscape scenes. The backs of enamel plates may even bear a ruby-coloured enamel reminiscent again of the porcelain examples, or else the whole surface may be elaborately decorated. The Ch'ien-lung 99 reign mark appears frequently, but no pieces are known with the Yung-chêng mark.

Apart from the dishes and plates, shapes also reflect foreign demand for the ware and include tea-caddies, ewers, plaques painted with Western scenes, vases with European figures and even candelabras. At the end of the 18th century and into the 19th century there is a decline in colour quality. Pale blue seems the dominant colour and designs become simpler. A vast quantity of this painted enamel is still made in China, in both Peking and Canton.

Japanese Enamels

Japanese enamel work, largely cloisonné, differs in many ways from its Chinese counterpart. Cloisonné is assumed to have arrived late in Japan, during the early 17th century, and during the late 18th century, at a time when it had become popular, a family called Hirata became proficient in the art. Sword furniture was a natural medium for enamelling, and sword guards (*tsuba*) are perhaps the best examples of this type, though whole sword scabbards are also known to have been enamelled. In the decoration of the *tsuba*, translucent enamels were made up in small medallions of gold or silver gilt and cemented or pressed into recesses in the sword fittings.

Other pieces that date from about the middle of the 18th century are somewhat cruder in execution. One type is of cast bronze decorated in champlevé with opaque enamels. This group, known as *hirado*, is supposed to be derived from Korean work.

The manufacture of cloisonné vessels as opposed to small decorative articles appears to have taken place later. Bowls, vases and boxes, with crowded floral designs, probably of the mid 19th century, were greatly admired by Western collectors in the latter years of the 19th century, as were Sátsuma ceramic wares. The colours are dull, however, lacking the brightness of the Chinese enamel colours, and the patterns are repetitive.

At the end of the 19th century a new school flourished in Kyoto which introduced precision wares in a variety of enamel colours. Such pieces are generally decorated with plants, flowers, birds and butterflies, and the treatment, though almost as delicate as that of any painted enamel, is still a cloisonné technique. A process 100, 102 which involved the removal of the wires before firing was also practised, and another variation, known in the West as '*plique à jour*', in which the enamels have no base and are translucent, gives an attractive appearance. 103 Cloisonné techniques were also applied to porcelain from about the mid 19th century, when the wires were cemented to a fired porcelain base, filled with the glass paste and refired. Naturalistic themes were also popular decorative subjects for this group.

LACQUER

Chinese Lacquer

Lacquer means many things to many people. In its Japanese form, delicately sprinkled with gold fragments, it may signify to the collector the world of tiny medicine boxes or *inro*. In its carved form it is associated with Chinese cinnabar trays, as well as boxes and vessels of the Ming and Ch'ing periods, carved with infinite patience. In the West it is thought of as shellac or the result of 'japanning' wood and dusting it with gold powder or gilding it with gold leaf.

Oriental lacquer is the juice of the tree *Rhus vernificera*, which is native to the countries of east Asia but may once have had a much wider distribution. When in use it displays remarkable properties; contact with moisture hardens it, and it has a high resistance to heat and acids. This hard lacquer can crack, but when it has been built up in tens or even hundreds of coats, each ground down in turn, it exhibits immense toughness. The foundation may sometimes be metal or fabric, but it is most commonly a soft, even-grained pine wood, carved to the right shape and sanded carefully to provide a flawless surface for the lacquering.

Chinese lacquer artefacts date from at least the late Chou dynasty (c. 400 BC), as evidenced by vessels and grave furniture from tomb excavations. Until the 10th century AD it was essentially a Chinese craft, yielding a range of techniques such as painted and inlaid work using gold, silver and mother-of-pearl, and in the 8th century three-dimensional carving. By the 10th century the Japanese had formed a style of their own. From the 13th century onwards, the lacquer wares of Korea and the Ryŭkyŭ Islands, as well as of Burma, Cambodia, Thailand and Vietnam, came into their own, though they were always closely connected with Chinese practice.

Techniques of working lacquer are very varied. Designs can be applied with a brush, plastic lacquer can be used as a mounting for other materials, or hard lacquer can be carved to produce deep relief, perhaps exposing different colour bands. Designs can be etched with a needle and filled with gold, or solid lacquer can be carved out and filled with plastic lacquer in another colour.

Lacquerware of the last three centuries BC consists of tomb accessories such as wine cups, toilet articles and trays painted with designs imitating the geometric styles of the late Chou dynasty, and a type of dragon scroll. Of course these are rare (as is all lacquer work before the Ming dynasty), but Sung pieces are often represented in museums and their vessel shapes are apparently related to ceramic shapes of the period.

To many collectors, carved lacquer is perhaps the most characteristic Chinese work and the supreme achievement in the craft from the 14th century onwards. Most of it is coloured with cinnabar, giving tints ranging from crimson to sealing-wax red. Up to two hundred layers of lacquer may have been applied, and individually rubbed down, before the carver starts the decoration. Carved red lacquer was made extensively in the 14th century and like blue and white porcelain reached a peak in the first half of the 15th century. With its floral, landscape and dragon designs, carved red lacquer owes little to its colour but a great deal to the ornate quality of its carving, a challenge met to the full in objects of large surface area such as trays, dishes and even tables.

Positive dating of individual pieces is not easy. Many pieces marked with dynasty and reign dates can be assumed to have been made under patronage at specially designated workshops. The only known dated pieces of the 15th century belong to the reigns of Yung-lo (1403–24) and Hsüan-tê (1426–35). As with porcelains and enamels made to official order, there was an imperial/official preference for certain types of decoration. In the 15th century, favoured lacquer themes were floral or figural, or arrangements of dragons and phoenixes. The best-known examples of floral themes are found on round shallow cylindrical boxes. A feature that helps to date these is a thin line of black lacquer, barely perceptible in the depth of the carving, which served as a marker for the carver to indicate the extent to which he could penetrate the layers with his relief design. Figural decoration depicts legendary or historical themes; open grounds in the design are filled with diaper patterns, the various motifs signifying air, water or earth.

From the reign of Chia-ching (1522–66) until the end of the reign of Wan-li (1573–1619) dated pieces again occur, though less commonly in the intervening Lung-ch'ing period (1567–72). Official wares of the Chia-ching period again show a preference for dragon designs, but also emblems, such as peaches, bearing auspicious characters. Convoluted dragons, perhaps slightly stiffer than their 15th-century counterparts, and elaborate phoenixes embellish many official Wan-li wares; treatment of floral panels is much more perfunctory. During the 16th century layers of lacquer of different colours began to be used which, when carved, gave a polychrome effect; most of such pieces are thought to have come from imperial workshops. Non-official wares consisted of a series of small round boxes, cylindrical or oval in vertical section and beautifully carved with floral or fruiting sprays. Small studies of two sages in a landscape scene belong to this group, as do rectangular boxes with similar designs fitted with an interior tray. Other types include rounded bowls and bowlstands, and stem cups with deep carving and key-fret foot rims.

Some of the most readily collectable pieces belong to the 18th century, when, as with porcelain and enamels, lacquer of the period reflects the rich embellished style and prodigious output of the reign of Ch'ien-lung (1736–95). Box-shapes appear frequently, some with metal foundations, some peach-shaped, as well as sweetmeat boxes with multiple nested trays, furniture 105 and even plaques. Apart from formal landscapes and ornamental gardens, and dragon/phoenix themes which

may bear the Ch'ien-lung mark, the preference appears to have been for scenes—for example, sages in a rocky landscape or detailed studies of 'a hundred boys' in a pavilion garden, or even well-known literary figures or Taoist immortals grouped to make a picture, all executed in crisp sharp carving. Covered bowls and round boxes in red lacquer fluted with radiating petals were much favoured by the Ch'ien-lung court, and can be dated to the late 18th century.

In some eyes, lacquer work inlaid with mother-of-pearl is only slightly less regarded. It is often mounted on a dark brown or black background, and its visual appeal is one of richness and delicacy combined with a wealth of decorative subjects and motifs. The best pieces are boxes and trays of the 16th and 17th centuries. Early work relies for its effect on colour variations of the shell, which may itself be incised to add detail; in later 108 pieces (18th and 19th centuries) the practice of tinting the underside of the shell gave rise to shades of pink, green, blue and purple that provide brilliant contrasts on a dark ground but lack the subtlety of early pieces. Sets 109 of small round dishes with tiny florette borders, central scenes of ladies in a pavilion, or legendary figures, are common, and even stem cups were made. A peculiar feature of Chinese mother-of-pearl work was the use of finely twisted wire to strengthen the edges of the work.

106 Chinese Coromandel lacquer screen showing ten panels decorated with figures in scenes in a palace garden; the border is decorated with flowers and antiques. The back of the screen bears a long dedicatory inscription dated 1718.

107 Detail of the Coromandel screen (106).

108 Chinese black lacquer tray with inlaid mother-of-pearl decoration. The robes of the dignitaries show the intricate incised designs on the shell; the deer in the foreground is an auspicious symbol auguring 'increased emolument'. 16th century.

Types of lacquer work other than carved red and mother-of-pearl inlay are too numerous to be covered here. One type, popular at the imperial court during the 16th century, appears on superficial examination to have been painted, but the effect has been achieved by carving out parts of the designs, filling them with coloured lacquer of other shades, and rubbing down the background and inlay to a uniform level, the outlines of the design then being incised and filled with gold. In this case the extent of deception matches the skill and virtuosity of the craftsman.

Lacquer was first exported in quantity to the West during the 17th century. It included 'Coromandel' lacquer which became popular in the form of cabinets, table tops, mirror frames, and folding screens, often as large as 8 ft high by 21 ft long. 'Coromandel' here signified only that the pieces had been imported to Europe via the Coromandel coast of India. The screens were made up of panels of pinewood cut in vertical sections and pinned with dowels. Layers of black lacquer over a white clay-like base were carved through, appropriate parts being decorated with various pigments and gold. Often central panels displayed garden scenes and had elaborate borders of flowers and 'antiques'. In Europe many screens were cut up into panels for smaller furniture, often without understanding of the subject decoration.

Japanese Lacquer

Lacquer wares are known to have been made in Japan in the 7th century, but the 'gold sprinkled' (*maki-e*) decoration, the special Japanese style that appears to owe nothing to China, evolved in the 10th century and from then on formed the basis of Japan's unique contribution to the art. *Maki-e* work of earlier centuries had great formal elegance and refined nuances of colour, but it is so rare that it is only likely to be found in the major museums. Its fullest expression in range of techniques and forms occurred in the 18th century, not only in small boxes (*inro*) but also in larger types—picnic boxes, writing boxes, etc.—whose subject matter included Japanese flowers of almost every kind, and also legends and scenes of everyday life.

The term *maki-e* denotes the scattering of gold or silver dust on a lacquer ground to create a design. Different ways of applying the metal dust produce a different effect, each given its own name. Of the more common techniques *maki-e* is essentially one of building up the design by repeated applications of lacquer alternated with sprinkling metal dust on the surface and rubbing it down. The design is achieved by the sprinkling rather than the painting. Although the surface is flat, a convincing sense of depth is achieved by delicate and graduated shading of the gold and silver dust.

Hira-maki-e ('flat sprinkled picture') is the name applied to all gold lacquer which has a flat surface (that is, in which the design itself is almost level with the background). The outline is transferred from a design on specially prepared paper; then the spaces enclosed by the transferred design are filled with an undercoating of lacquer on to which gold powder is dusted. Repeated

109 Chinese black lacquer bowl portraying figures in an ornamental garden in tinted mother-of-pearl. 17th or 18th century.

110 Japanese lacquer treasure box, here showing the inside of the lid with the design in sprinkled gold (*maki-e*) on a brownish black ground; the scene depicts a Japanese legend centred around a fisherman Urashima. Late Heian or early Kamakura period, 12th century. Seattle Art Museum (gift of the late Mrs D. E. Frederick).

111 Japanese lacquer writing box. The design is evocative of the fall of blossom at Shirakawa. 15th century. Nezu Institute of Fine Arts, Tokyo.

112 Chinese lacquer tray carved in V-shaped grooves through layers of black and red lacquer to a buff ground, the central scrolls representing sceptre heads. 16th century.

113 Japanese *inro. top right* Two-case *Kinji* (literally 'gold-ground'), with metal applique, depicting the poetess Ono Komachi washing her book of poems; the background is influenced by the Toza school of painting; early 19th century. *top left* Four-case *Kinji*, with fan-shaped panels of birds, flowers and foliage in Shiboyama style; early 19th century. *below* Four-case *Roiro* (black lacquer ground), with waterfall and rocks in *aogai* (blue-green seashell) and gold *taka-maki-e*; the reverse shows a writer's table, book and implements; signed Soetsu in his 82nd year; early 18th century.

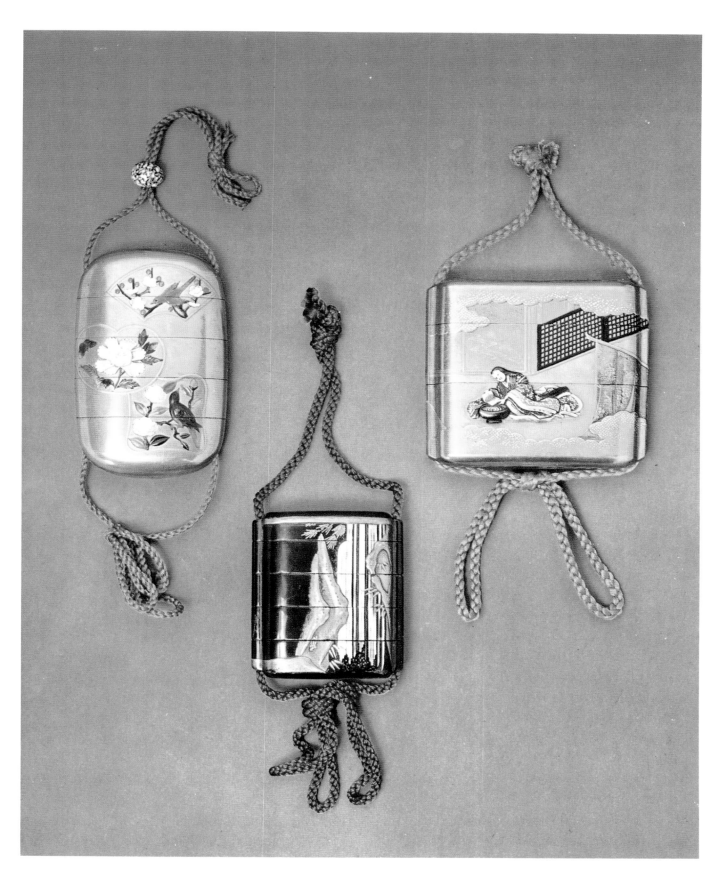

graduated dustings account for the final effect, in which the outlines and often the details are very slightly raised.

113   *Taka-maki-e* ('raised sprinkled picture') describes all raised gold lacquer. It may include the inlaying of thin metal or mother of pearl flakes. The technique is used for near perspective such as figures, rocks and trees. The design is again transferred from paper and the special undercoat lacquer applied. Repeated applications, typical of the sheer labour of lacquer work, are then made, along with the addition of such other materials as are necessary for the design. Then the final details are added as in *hira-maki-e*, and the final coat applied.

Togidashi ('appearing by rubbing') is used in combination with raised lacquer to achieve subtle effects of distance such as mists, clouds and mountain tops. The design is transferred from paper or, in more recent times, drawn directly with white lead. After repeated applications of lacquer, each followed by grinding down, the final effect is absolutely even, with the gold dust design emerging through the black lacquer.

Background for designs may be a wooden base of ornamental woods or cherry bark with the lacquer design directly applied. The natural grain can be brought out with transparent lacquer. Lacquer could also be made to simulate metal, wood or pottery, but backgrounds usually consisted of black, gold or red lacquer. Many other decorative techniques were employed including encrusting designs with mother-of-pearl, tortoiseshell, ivory, coral, wood, porcelain, malachite and soapstone. Metal foil was often placed under the translucent tortoiseshell to enhance its appearance.

Lacquer carved in formal repetitive scrolls through layers of different colours was popular in 18th- and 19th-century Japan, especially for the smaller objects. Known in modern times as *guri* ('crooked ring'), the technique was derived from China, where it held an important place in lacquer art from the 8th century to the end of the
112 Ming period.

However, the widest range of Japanese lacquer techniques is displayed in the small lacquer boxes known
113 as *inro*. Ostensibly used for pills or powders, they are small (approximately $3\frac{1}{2} \times 2 \times 1$ in.) and are divided into several hollow sections. They were suspended by a silk cord hidden under the sash, and came into general use as an article of dress at the end of the 16th century. The *netsuke*, or small ornamental carving, was attached at the other end of the cord. Most *inro* had a wood or leather foundation coated with lacquer which may be decorated in any of the methods mentioned above. All sides and all parts of the *inro* are finished including the insides, which often show a fine use of coloured lacquer of red, black or gold.

Lacquer pieces were not signed with any regularity until the early 17th century. Early works commissioned by court or officials did not carry signatures, but when *inro* were more generally owned, signed works were considered proper. Almost all the great lacquer artists we know of made *inro*, sometimes even combining their talents on one piece, as evidenced by two signatures. Nevertheless, it is extremely difficult to verify the authenticity of a signature. Two families famous for *inro* work are Kajikawa and Koma, both active between the 17th and 19th centuries. Ranking among foremost individual artists are Zeshin (1807–91), Shiomi Masanari (1647–1725) and Yoyusai (1772–1845).

Korean and Ryŭkyŭ Lacquer

The Korean and Ryŭkyŭ lacquer arts made a significant contribution to the Oriental achievement. A special feature of Ryŭkyŭ work is the use of a red lacquer ground in combination with mother-of-pearl decoration, but its mother-of-pearl inlay on black lacquer has distinction as great as any produced by its two neighbours, Japan and China.

Korean lacquers inlaid with mother-of-pearl achieved considerable distinction as early as the Koryō dynasty (AD 932–1392). Fine scroll work was done using silver alloy wire and tortoiseshell in the design. Large pieces of mother-of-pearl made up the more simple designs of the 14th and 15th centuries, while the box shown here is an example of the late 18th-century use of more formal designs in which twisted wires are employed within the design for the stems of the open lotus.

111

SMALL CARVINGS

Chinese Ivory Carvings

The term 'ivory' embraces a variety of materials from which carvings are made. Usually they are of elephant or walrus tusk and easily worked; the only limitation is the dimension of the tusk which rarely exceeds 7 in. in diameter. Nevertheless, its close grain, natural lustre and satin smoothness have made it a preferred material for smaller objects such as figures, Japanese *netsuke*, and objects for the scholar's table.

Some early small carvings, for example pins, fish-hooks, beads and finials, carry designs closely resembling those on bronzes of the Shang and Chou periods; they are thought to be of ivory though they may contain pieces of bone. From the 10th century China's maritime trade centred round the port of Ch'üan-chou, which was

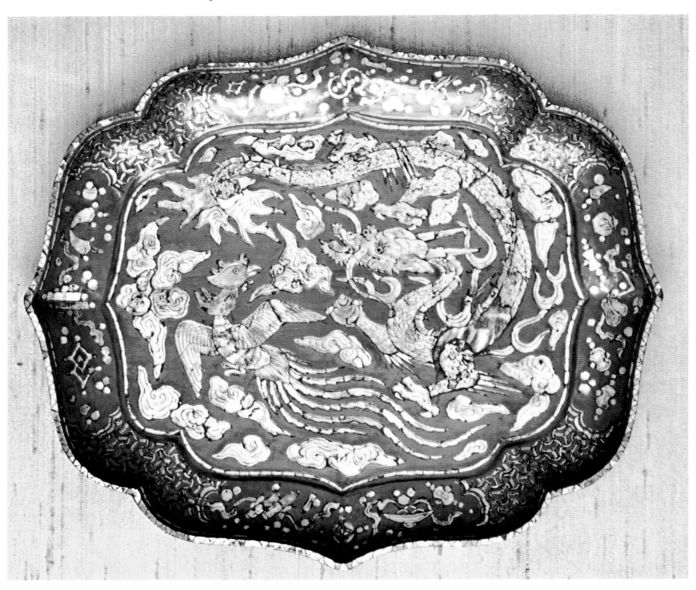

115 Ryŭkyŭan red lacquer tray with inlaid mother-of-pearl decoration showing a phoenix and a dragon clutching a pearl; the border bears a design of the Taoist emblems. 17th century.

116 Chinese carving of a dignitary holding a gemstone. 17th century.

visited regularly by Arab traders, then the custodians of the ivory trade. Trade between China and Africa was established in the early years of the Ming dynasty, and carved ivories attributed to the later years of the Ming are numerous, especially the long graceful carved figures retaining the natural lines of the tusk. The output of the Ch'ing dynasty was prodigious, and a fine example of imperial ware is the brushpot which bears the Ch'ien-lung seal mark on its base.

The most commonly found carvings for the home market are combs, backscratchers, mah-jong sets, chop-sticks, girdle pendants, and numerous articles for the use of the opium smoker and the scholar. Foremost among the latter are the little ivory screens which stood on the scholar's table. Carvings for export to the West, a trade covering two centuries, included carved ivory trinkets, fans, brushes, glove boxes, tea-caddies and gambling counters. Perhaps the most delicate workmanship was that of the fans, each fold carved through in openwork designs of floral or landscape scenes.

Chinese ivories are rarely signed and thus cannot easily be dated. Ivory work which appears beautifully browned and mellow may not be old, especially since there are time-honoured methods of promoting such appearance. It should be remarked also that carvings easily available in Hong Kong, the nested balls and curved-hull boats with hundreds of occupants, although marvels of technical skill, show a precision absent in older works.

Chinese Wood Carvings

The most readily collectable wood carvings are appur-tenances for the scholar's table or come under the head-ing of miniature arts. These are the small articles carved in box wood, willow or bamboo. Some of the finest carvings of small figures, wrist-rests or brushwashers have been made in bamboo, though passing mention should be made of a certain Hsia Pai-yen who is reported to have carved on an olive stone sixteen frogs, each with a distinctive face.

The hollow stem of the bamboo lends itself to the making of wrist-rests and brushpots, which were carved on the outside in relief, or occasionally in open-work design, with foliage, mountains, rocky crags, hidden pavilions, etc. Sometimes the reverse of the brushpot would bear a poem incised in the wood. Unlike much carved work, many of these bamboo carv-ings are signed. Although such carvers' names are recorded as far back as the Sung dynasty, it is safest to assume that the majority of carvings surviving today are products of the 18th and 19th centuries. The set of musicians illustrated all bear the mark of the same carver.

117 Chinese ivory brushpot modelled on the ancient bronze *ku* form and bearing archaistic motifs – the monster mask (*t'ao-t'ieh*) and the 'thunder pattern' background. Ch'ien-lung period, 1736–95.

118 Chinese brushwasher carved from a bamboo root and formed as a gnarled pine branch. 18th or 19th century.

Japanese Netsuke

A form of Oriental miniature carving which has enchanted many collectors in the West is that of Japanese *netsuke*, which were produced in great numbers in the 18th and 19th centuries. By the beginning of the 20th century large collections were being formed, some of which, such as the Goncourt collection, have become renowned.

The *netsuke* is generally a small three-dimensional carving measuring between 1 and 2½ in., usually in wood or ivory, and representing a small figure, a utilitarian object, a button-like object or a box. Like *inro* it had a practical purpose, that of suspending keys or other articles within one's clothes, the kimono having no pockets. The subject matter of these small carvings is very wide, falling into several categories: the *manju*, shaped like a round Japanese bun; the *kata-bori*, figures of humans and animals, including various types of dolls, puppets, and Noh dancers; utilitarian *netsuke* such as seals (*ing yo*), abacus (*soroban*) and sundials (*hidokei*);

and other forms including the basketwork *netsuke* of metal or rattan, as well as trick *netsuke* such as self-righting figures.

Most *netsuke* were made of wood and ivory, but rhinoceros horn, shell and ceramics were also used. Often the wood was stained, painted or lacquered. Sometimes different parts would be made of different materials. A wooden torso may have an ivory face and hands, and a silver hat. Some artists specialised in portraying particular animals, many of which would have had a symbolical or mythological meaning. But figures were generally depicted in a life-like manner.

Difficulties exist in interpreting signatures on *netsuke*, since the same signature could be used by the descendants of the original master. The style of the carving and the type and quality of the material have to be assessed as well as the authenticity of the signature. In fact, a *netsuke* is best chosen for its artistry, its interesting subject matter, its craftsmanship, and then only for its signature. The deciding factor must of course be the personal taste of the collector.

THE WORLD OF COLLECTORS

Collectors participate in a world of dealers, auctioneers, museum curators, craftsmen and other collectors, all of whom depend on one another, and all of whom contribute to the continuous process of uncovering, identifying, appreciating and publicising man's artistic and cultural achievements. There is no culture, no artefact, no creation of craftsmanship and beauty with which collectors are not associated. Indeed, in many cases they lead in the discovery and delineation of yet another area of man's projection of himself, and the objects of beauty and utility through which it is expressed.

To the novice collector of Oriental antiques the range of objects, and the time span of their production, must seem daunting. Nevertheless his range of interest will be narrowed by his motives for collecting. If it is the sheer antiquity of certain classes of objects, he will find his attention drawn to neolithic pottery, jade or ancient bronzes. If form and shape and their process of development are important, then ancient ritual vessels will attract him. Or it may be technological aspects, technical 'firsts' in craftsmanship as in the earliest porcelain. Perhaps an affinity for the culture—the closed world of Chinese art—may lead him to collect across periods and across materials. A particular quality of life or form of society as expressed in the art objects of the period may dictate his field of interest. Alternatively, pure aesthetics may impel him to search for colours and decorations conforming to his estimation of good taste, leading him to discriminate between bright, colourful decoration on the one hand and 'classic', simple and subtle on the other; between Ch'ing porcelain and Sung ceramics. And finally for some, in addition to these motivations, there will be the excitement of studying prices, buying 'wisely' and excusing the expenditure on grounds of investment.

A starting point for the new collector, and an ever useful frame of reference, is the museum collection. Objects may be studied and returned to for comparison, and the serious regular visitor will be able to make contact with the staff. Museum staff will generally authenticate objects brought to them but will not estimate values. In the larger museums the exhibits are often outstanding examples, and may be exceptional in comparison with those in circulation among dealers and collectors. In many cases more mundane examples will be held in the museum's reserve collection in rooms not normally open to the casual visitor. Such reserve collections are often rotated with the objects on public display, but it can take several years for the cycle to be completed. Because collections in some major museums are almost fully representative of certain classes of objects, booklets published by museums are authoritative, and often cheap.

A new collector is well advised to make his first purchases from reputable dealers. They will recommend that he should buy the best condition of object for the money available, as an object in perfect condition will always be a greater asset than one of comparable price, higher artistic quality, but showing more wear or damage. Dealers may be used for bidding at auctions, and their advice on authenticity, assessment of damage and guidance as to value will more than compensate for the commission they charge. Serious collectors will find it advantageous to subscribe to the catalogues of the leading auction houses, and to the post-sale price lists that are circulated.

A large proportion of dealers' stock is purchased at auction. Occasionally items are bought from other dealers or private individuals. Although a private individual may be tempted to visit several dealers with a view to obtaining the highest possible price for his object, he should exercise some discretion and not attempt to play off one dealer against another. A dealer may sometimes offer for sale a complete collection or a substantial part of one, selling it on a commission basis on behalf of the owner. Such sales may sometimes be combined into an exhibition which not only affords a unique opportunity to observe the theme of acquisition and taste of a major collector, but also provides an exhibition catalogue which may be an important record of a coherent group of objects, thereafter dispersed into the hands of a number of collectors or museums.

A collector may wish to sell an item at auction rather than through a dealer, and indeed a dealer may sometimes advise him to do this. One advantage of selling at auction lies in the fact that an object may benefit by being placed in an important sale. Conversely, a disadvantage is that if an object does not reach its agreed reserve price, it may be 'bought in' by the auctioneers, whereupon the seller must pay a percentage of the final bid offered. Unfortunately it is often the case with such 'bought in' pieces that although they may be offered

119 Chinese bamboo brushpot carved with an openwork design of scholars and attendants examining a scroll beneath rocky crags and pines. 18th or 19th century.

again at the next suitable sale, the fact that they have failed once does not augur well for the next time.

The collector is cautious by nature and the discovery of cleverly concealed restoration work is his forte. A crack in a ceramic object may have been concealed not just by a tiny application of paint but sometimes by having the whole area in the vicinity of the crack 'painted out'. Breaks or damage in bronze may have been treated in the same way, such restoration only being detected conclusively by an ultra-violet lamp. In extreme cases of doubt about authenticity, scientific analysis may be brought to bear, the most publicised being the thermoluminescence testing of pottery. Dealers or museums can give details of where to obtain such a service.

Oriental art is particularly renowned for its 'licence to imitate'. Throughout Chinese art imitations have been perpetuated in a spirit of innocence, respect or desire to please, but downright forgeries have been produced as well. Investigation of shapes, designs and techniques known to date to specific cultural periods is now sorting out the long lines of tradition as well as the geographical location of materials. The intense activity in this field by scholar collectors, such as Sir Harry Garner, is respon-

121 Japanese *netsuke. left* Ivory *netsuke*, Kyoto school: standing *ama* or diving girl in grass skirt holding a sickle. 18th century. *centre* Wood mask of a grinning demon, signed Ichiryusai. 19th century. *right* Ivory *netsuke*, Osaka school: group of two rats with inlaid eyes. 19th century.

122 Chinese bamboo carvings of the Eight Immortals, each with their attributes; each figure bears the same carver's mark. 18th or 19th century.

sible for a considerable area of our knowledge of these anomalies.

Dealers may be approached about restoration or repair work. It is notoriously slow, and the collector must be content to release his possession for some months. It goes without saying that fine antiques require careful handling. Bronzes, especially those with a fine patination, should be handled as little as possible, but in contrast ivory benefits from constant handling, becoming more mellow in colour in the course of time. Woods, lacquers and ivories may crack in dry heat, and inlaid mother-of-pearl can be dislodged easily with the wipe of a duster. To some collectors of Chinese bronzes the patina can be of considerable importance, since the effects of burial in certain conditions may bring about a crusty or powdery surface of green, blue or purplish tints. Nevertheless, a harmful form of patination is 'bronze disease', which is indicated by light green spots within the patination and needs expert treatment.

The hazards of collecting enumerated may seem somewhat sobering, but the collector will find that consulting dealers, visiting the great museum collections and pursuing his own reading will guide him wisely and provide an enjoyment and excitement second to none.

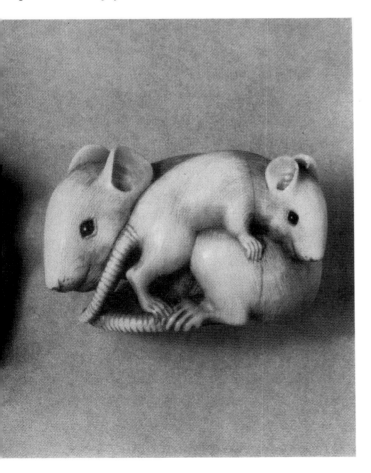

APPENDIX

Comparative Chronologies

Thailand (styles)	China	Dates	Japan	Korea
	Neolithic period	c. 7000–c. 1600 BC		
	Shang dynasty	c. 1600–1027 BC		
	Western Chou dynasty	1027–770 BC		
		c. 1000–200 BC	Jōmon period	
	Period of the Spring and Autumn Annals	770–475 BC		
	Warring States	475–221 BC		
	Ch'in dynasty	221–207 BC		
	Western Han dynasty	206–AD 8		
		c. 200–AD 500	Yayoi period	
		c. 57 BC–AD 668		Silla period
	Hsin dynasty (Wang Mang)	AD 9–23		
	Eastern Han dynasty	24–220		
	Six Dynasties	221–589		
		c. 300–c. 700	Tumulus period	
Dvāravatī		500–1100		
		538–645	Asuka (Suiko) period	
	Sui dynasty	581–618		
	T'ang dynasty	618–906		
		645–712	Hakuhō period	
		668–935		Greater Silla Empire
Śrīvijaya		700–1300		
		710–784	Nara period	
		794–876	Early Heian period	
		895–1185	Fujiwara (Late Heian) period	
	Five Dynasties	907–960		
	Liao dynasty	907–1125		
		932–1392		Koryō period
	Sung dynasty	960–1279		
Lopburî		1000–1400		
Chieng Sèn		1100–1950		
Û Tòng		1100–1500		
		1185–1392	Kamakura period	
Sukhodaya		1200–1500		
	Yüan dynasty	1280–1368		
		1338–1573	Muromachi (Ashikaga) period	
	Ming dynasty	1368–1644		
		1392–1910		Yi dynasty
Ayudhyā		1400–1800		
		1568–1615	Momoyama period	
		1615–1868	Tokugawa (Edo) period	
	Ch'ing dynasty	1644–1912		
Bangkok		1700–1950		
		1868–1912	Meiji period	

Chinese Reign Marks

Chinese reign marks, used during the Ming and Ch'ing dynasties, were added to articles made in porcelain, lacquer, enamel, ivory and bronze, being incised, cast, painted or inlaid. Sometimes they were used 'out of period' when an earlier style was being imitated. They were also used when an earlier reign mark was added to a later work with intent to deceive, or when a production or quality was deemed to merit the mark of a reign famous for superior craftsmanship.

123 Reign Period Marks–Ming Dynasty

Hung-wu
1368–98

Yung-lo
1403–24

Yung-lo
1403–24

Hsüan-tê
1426–35

Ch'êng-hua
1465–87

Hung-chih
1488–1505

Chêng-tê
1506–21

Chia-ching
1522–66

Lung-ch'ing
1567–72

Wan-li
1573–1619

T'ien-ch'i
1621–27

Ch'ung-chên
1628–43

124 Reign Period Marks–Ch'ing Dynasty

Shun-chih 1644–61

K'ang-hsi 1662–1722

Yung-chêng 1723–35

Ch'ien-lung 1736–95

Chia-ch'ing 1796–1820

Tao-kuang 1821–50

Hsien-fêng 1851–61

T'ung-chih 1862–73

Kuang-hsü 1874–1908

Hsüan-t'ung 1909–12

Hung-hsien 1916 (Yüan shih-k'ai)

The Bronze Ritual Vessels

125 Food cookers

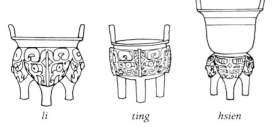

li   ting   hsien

126 Food containers

tou   kuei

127 For ceremonial ablutions

chien   p'an

128 Water or wine containers

yü   hu   lei   fang-i

129 Wine goblets

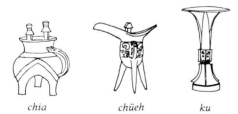

chia   chüeh   ku

130 Wine servers

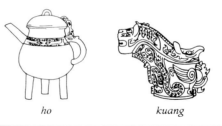

ho   kuang

Some Early Jade Shapes

131 *Tsung*, a ritual jade commonly regarded as an earth symbol; halberd, a ritual jade called a *ko* which became a badge of rank; *kuei*, a form of sceptre, an emblem of office or badge of rank; sword furniture: the guard, the chape, the sling fitting.

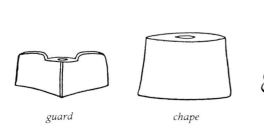

guard   chape   sling fitting

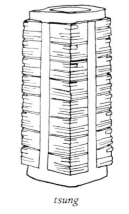

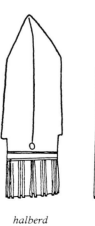

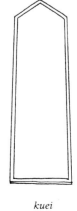

tsung   halberd   kuei

132 Standing and seated positions (asana): *samabhanga*, upright and standing; *tribhanga*, 'three ways bent', typical of Bodhisattvas of Indian, East Asian and Lamaist origin: *âlîdha*, 'lunging' position; *pratyâlîdha-tandava*, stance of wild looking female gods, Dakini or Yogini; *vajrâsana*, the 'Diamond Position' or 'Lotus Position'; *mahârâja-lîlâ*, position of 'Royal Ease', characteristic of the Bodhisattva Avalokiteśvara; *lalitâsana*, typical of female deities and some Bodhisattvas; *bhadrâsana*, 'European' manner, typical for Maitreya Buddha.

samabhanga *tribhanga* *âlîdha* *pratyâlîdha-tandava* *vajrâsana* *mahârâja-lîlâ* *lalitâsana* *bhadrâsana*

133 Position of hands (mudrâ): *abhaya*, 'Freedom from fear'; *âdarśa*, usually related to the Goddess Vasundharâ, but rare; *anjali*, 'worshipping' usually seen in supporting figures, Ananda, Mahakasyapa, the Buddha's disciples; *bhavishya-vyâkarana*, 'prophecy of the future' seen in Śakyamuni figures, but rare; *bhûmisparśa*, 'earth touching', the seated Buddha calling the earth to witness his victory over temptation; *dharmaçakra*, 'turning the wheel of instruction', symbolic of the first teaching of the Buddha; *dhyâna*, 'meditation', characteristic of Amitabha Buddha; *karana*, 'fulfilment'; *kshepana*, 'sprinkling with holy water' hands pendent over holy water bottle, typical of Bodhisattva Nâmasangîti; *lola-hasta*, loose pendent hand; *namaskâra*, 'veneration'; *tarjani*, 'warning'; *tarpana*, 'satiety', veneration for dead ancestors; *vajrahûmkâra*, 'The Diamond and Hum Sutra', usually seen in Adi-Buddhas and mystical deities in union with a Sakti; *varada*, 'bestowing'; *vitarka* or *vyâkarana*, 'discussion'.

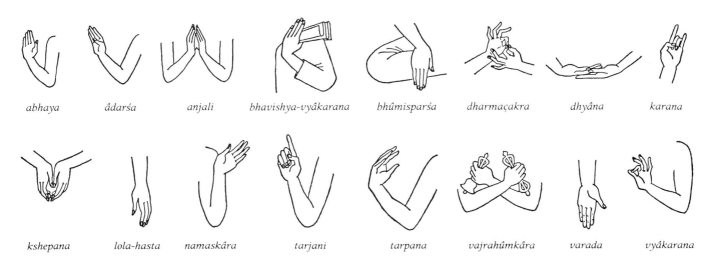

abhaya *âdarśa* *anjali* *bhavishya-vyâkarana* *bhûmisparśa* *dharmaçakra* *dhyâna* *karana*

kshepana *lola-hasta* *namaskâra* *tarjani* *tarpana* *vajrahûmkâra* *varada* *vyâkarana*

Decorative Motifs

134 Eight Buddhist Emblems. *left to right* The wheel; the conch shell; the umbrella; the canopy; the lotus; the vase; the paired fish; the endless knot.

These often appear on later ceramics, lacquer and cloisonné and after the Ming dynasty may be replaced or added to by some of the Taoist emblems.

135 Eight Precious Things. *left to right* The jewel; the cash; the open lozenge; the pair of books; the solid lozenge; the musical stone; the pair of horns; the artemisia leaf.

These motifs, particularly prevalent on porcelain, may also appear individually as base marks, especially the last mentioned, on porcelain of the K'ang-hsi period (1662–1722).

136 Eight Taoist Emblems. *left to right* The gourd; the fan; the flower basket; the rods and drum; the lotus; the sword; the flute; the castanets.

Each emblem is carried by one of the Taoist Immortals: Li T'ieh-kuai (gourd), friend of Lao Tz'u, represented as a lame beggar; Chung-li Ch'üan (fan), an immortalised Chou dynasty statesman with powers for reviving dead souls; Lan Ts'ai-ho (flower baskets), often represented as a woman, earns her living by singing in the streets; Chang-kuo Lao (rods and drum), a magician of 7th- or 8th-century fame, often shown accompanied by his mule; Ho Hsien-ku (lotus), daughter of a shopkeeper made famous in the 7th century for her long journeys on foot to gather bamboo shoots for her sick mother; Lü Tung-pin (sword), an 8th century scholar and recluse, the patron

immortal of barbers; Han Hsiang-tzǔ (flute), 9th-century nephew of the famous scholar Han Yü and the patron immortal of musicians, had power to make flowers grow instantaneously; Ts'ao Kuo-ch'iu (castanets), 10th-century son of a military commander and brother of a Sung dynasty empress, was the patron immortal of actors.

137 T'ao-t'ieh masks. Two of the many variations of the *t'ao-t'ieh* animal mask which is one of the most important decorative motifs appearing initially on early bronzes.

138 K'uei dragons. Another motif in early bronze ornament, these are dragon figures often appearing as supporting decoration to the *t'ao-t'ieh* mask.

BIBLIOGRAPHY

Ceramics

Ayers, John, *The Baur Collection*, 4 volumes, Geneva 1968
Garner, Sir Harry, *Oriental Blue and White*, London 1954
Gompertz, G. St G. M., *Chinese Celadon Wares*, London 1958
Honey, W. B., *The Ceramic Art of China and Other Countries of the Far East*, London 1944
Jenyns, R. S., *Later Chinese Porcelain*, London 1951
Medley, Margaret, *A Handbook of Chinese Art*, London 1964
Transactions of the Oriental Ceramic Society, London, annual volumes from 1921 onwards
Wirgin, Jan, *Sung Ceramic Designs*, Bulletin no. 42 of the Bulletins of the Museum of Far Eastern Antiquities, Stockholm 1970

Non-Ceramics

Garner, Sir Harry, *Chinese and Associated Lacquer from the Garner Collection*, British Museum, London, October–December 1973
Garner, Sir Harry, *Chinese and Japanese Cloisonné Enamels*, London 1962
Griswold, A. B., *et al.*, *Burma, Korea, Tibet*, 'Art of the World' series, London 1964
Hansford, S. H., *Chinese Carved Jades*, London 1968
Jahss, M. and B., *Inro and Other Miniature Forms of Japanese Lacquer Art*, London 1972
Jenyns, R. S., and W. Watson, *Chinese Art: The Minor Arts*, 2 volumes, London 1963
Watson, William, *Ancient Chinese Bronzes*, London 1962

ACKNOWLEDGMENTS

The Publishers are grateful for permission to reproduce drawings from the following books: Goepper, Roger, *Kunst und Kunsthandwerk Ostasiens*, Keyersche Verlagsbuchhandlung, Munich (132, 133); Medley, Margaret, *A Handbook of Chinese Art*, G. Bell & Sons Ltd, London (123–131, 134–138).

Unless otherwise stated all photographs in this publication were taken on behalf of the Hamlyn Publishing Group by Hawkley Studios Associates Ltd, at Messrs Bluett & Sons Ltd, 48 Davies Street, London W1. The remaining photographs were kindly provided by the following: H. Blairman & Son Ltd: 106, 107; Bluett & Sons Ltd: endpapers, contents page, 2, 6, 7, 8, 13, 18, 19, 30, 40, 45, 48, 65, 66, 70, 72, 74, 76, 78, 83, 85, 86, 90, 112, 115, 122; Cooper-Bridgeman Library: 37; J. Crichton: 51, 54; Hamlyn Group Picture Library: 3, 5, 20, 34, 46, 50, 53, 59, 60, 69, 71, 75, 79, 80, 84, 91, 100, 103, 110, 111, 114; Hugh M. Moss Ltd: 120; Sotheby & Co.: 10, 23, 25, 31, 32, 35; Victoria and Albert Museum, London: 9, 38, 41, 56, 60, 88, 91, 102; D. J. K. Wright Ltd: 113, 121.

INDEX

Figures in bold type refer to illustrations